RYA Yac
Te

by Jeremy Evans

Illustrator: Pete Galvin

© Jeremy Evans 2011
First Published 2011
Reprinted January 2018
The Royal Yachting Association
RYA House, Ensign Way, Hamble
Southampton SO31 4YA
Tel: 02380 604 100
Web: www.rya.org.uk

Follow us on Twitter @RYAPublications
or on YouTube

We welcome feedback on our
publications at publications@rya.org.uk

You can check content updates for
RYA publications at www.rya.org.uk/
go/bookschangelog

ISBN: 978-1-906435448
RYA Order Code: G94

*Sustainable
Forests*

A CIP record of this book is available from the British Library.

Note: While all reasonable care has been taken in the preparation
of this book, the publisher takes no responsibility for the use of the
methods or products or contracts described in the book.

Cover Design: Pete Galvin
Typesetting and Design: Kevin Slater
Proofreading and indexing: Alan Thatcher
Printed in China through World Print
Photo credits: Jeremy Evans, Chatham Deck Shoes,
Pains Wessex, www.simrad-yachting.com, Sunsail

INTRODUCTION

RYA Yacht Sailing Techniques provides a guide to some of the techniques you may need to assist you to enjoy sailing a small to medium-sized yacht safely. All of the techniques are suitable for relaxed cruising with a family, particularly flotilla or bareboat holidays in beautiful locations with guaranteed sun! The object is to make your next sailing holiday as enjoyable and stress-free as possible through being confident about being able to manage a yacht under sail or power, moored in a marina or lying at anchor. This is only a basic overview of yacht sailing techniques. For those who wish to increase their knowledge and expertise to higher levels, specialist RYA courses and books are recommended for all sections covered in this book.

Jeremy Evans

ACKNOWLEDGEMENTS

Thanks to Keith and Andrea Darbyshire who did a wonderful job running the Sunsail yacht school in Lanzarote. Thanks to Chris Satchwell for his help over many years at Sunsail. Thanks to Euan, Peter, Katrina, Andrew and Louise at Sunsail, Port Solent. Thanks to Pete Galvin for his excellent illustrations, to Kevin Slater for his great layouts and to Phil Williams-Ellis for being a most understanding editor.

Thanks to many owners who let me enjoy sailing their boats, including Shaun Webb (Bavaria 32), Nick Atkinson (Oceanis 393), Gavin and Nicky Howe (Swan 48), Nick and Catherine Madinaveitia (Hunter Legend 340) and Rod Carr (Broadblue 38). Thanks to all the friendly people who let me sail the superb Degero 36, Nauticat 351, Maestro 40, Finngulf 41 and 43 in the magnificent Finnish archipelago. Thanks to James and Jane Ellis for the loan of their magnificent Maxi 1100 Iona, fully fitted including Oscar the labrador, on the West Coast of Scotland and in the Shetlands.

Thanks to Bryony, Ivory and Ysemay for their great work on Sunfast yachts in Lanzarote.

CONTENTS

1 HOW TO ENJOY YACHT CRUISING

Why is yacht cruising so enjoyable? Because it combines the superb sensation of being driven across water by wind with the freedom to live and explore afloat. The weather may play an important role in your enjoyment, but without doubt the most fundamental requirement is being able to handle the yacht safely and securely in all situations.

RYA Yacht Sailing Techniques describes and illustrates the basic skills that are required to manage a yacht under sail or power, at rest in a marina or lying at anchor. It aims to provide enough information for you and your crew to enjoy yacht cruising in user-friendly conditions, which most of us would award a 'five star' rating. This means fair weather, light to moderate winds, little or no tide, a quiet sailing area, easily assessed navigational hazards, well protected anchorages with good holding and uncrowded marinas.

Although some of the factors may change, thankfully, it is possible to encounter such mellow conditions in many popular sailing areas. For instance, many of the photos for this book were shot in the Canaries, which ticked all those boxes during a week spent cruising around the south of the island of Lanzarote. However, we were fully aware that the same cruising area can also be extremely rough and windy, just as strong

tides can pose a challenge when sailing off the coastline of the UK.

Thousands of hours are required to build up experience afloat, and no matter how experienced the sailor there will always be more things to learn. In the meantime, RYA Yacht Sailing Techniques will help to start the ball rolling, building up expertise which should be enhanced by the RYA's Competent Crew and Day Skipper courses.

WHICH YACHT?

Some of the photos in this book were taken at Sunsail's Yacht Schools in Lanzarote and Port Solent. The Sun Fast 37 used at these schools is a typical modern cruising yacht with emphasis on good sailing performance. Differences in specification when compared to other yachts may require slightly different boat handling techniques. When differences are major, such as with mainsail reefing systems, the book illustrates other popular methods of yacht technique.

1

2 ON DECK

Much of your time afloat will be spent managing the yacht under sail or power from the comfort of the cockpit, with trips on deck for mooring, dropping anchor and hoisting or dropping the mainsail.

The Deck

2

Modern cruising yachts have similar deck layouts designed around a cockpit for the helmsman and crew, coachroof providing standing headroom in the main cabin area, side decks and foredeck for the crew to move around the boat when changing sails or mooring, transom with swimming platform and boarding ladder.

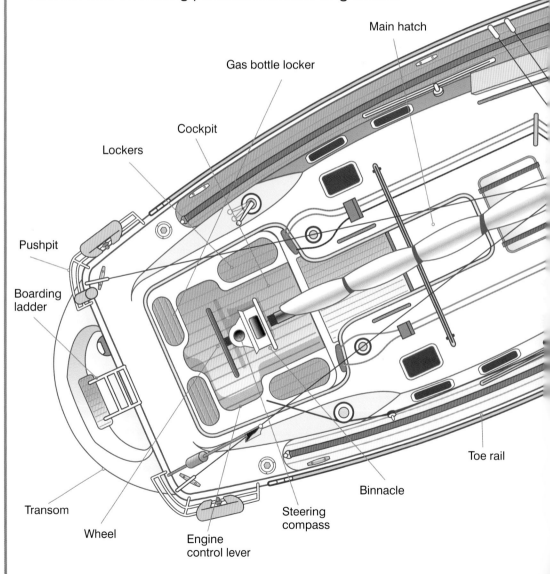

Main hatch

Gas bottle locker

Cockpit

Lockers

Pushpit

Boarding ladder

Transom

Wheel

Engine control lever

Steering compass

Binnacle

Toe rail

2

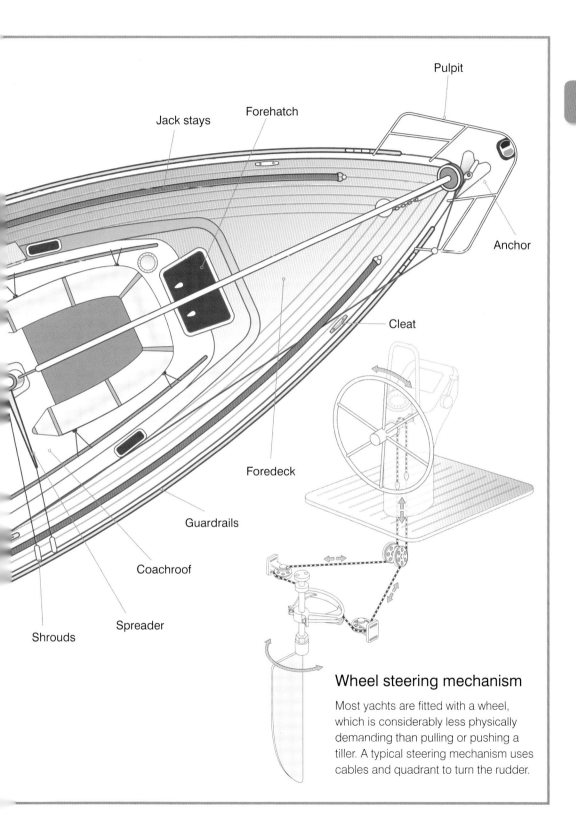

Pulpit

Jack stays

Forehatch

Anchor

Cleat

Foredeck

Guardrails

Coachroof

Spreader

Shrouds

Wheel steering mechanism

Most yachts are fitted with a wheel, which is considerably less physically demanding than pulling or pushing a tiller. A typical steering mechanism uses cables and quadrant to turn the rudder.

2

TRANSOM

The transom is the back end of the boat. On most cruising yachts, it is very wide because one or two cabins have been built into the stern. This provides plenty of space for the transom to incorporate a bathing platform and step ladder. On charter yachts it's normally complete with a pressurised shower hose. Stainless steel tubing with horizontal guardrails forms a pushpit which provides a fence around the transom, incorporating storage for man overboard safety equipment.

GETTING ON BOARD

For vessels moored stern-to, the easiest way to get on board is through the pushpit at the stern. Simply step onto the transom, unhook the guard rails and climb into the cockpit. If the stern is some way from the dock, it is safest to use a boarding plank. Make sure the plank is secured to the boat and has a large overlap on the dock.

For vessels secured alongside a dock or pontoon, you can step on from the side. At the mid-point of the yacht it's normally safest to step onto the aluminium (or teak) toe rail, which runs along the side of the boat. Grab the nearest shroud for support, while lifting your legs over the guardrails. A 'gate' is often provided by two narrowly spaced stanchions with guardrails unclipped so you can step on or off the dock. Use of this gate could be vital when recovering a man overboard.

The Finngulf 41 has a large scooped transom, providing a convenient boarding area from the dock or tender, as well as a convenient bathing platform.

COCKPIT

The cockpit is the main crew area when you are afloat. There should be sufficient space for everyone on board, though it may often be a squash. Cockpit seats are often contoured so you can sit comfortably when the boat is heeling – if there's space, it's best to sit on the windward (uphill) side.

If the boat has a sprayhood, use it to protect the crew from the effects of spray and wind chill. The disadvantage of a sprayhood is that it may impair the helm's forward vision and make it more difficult for the crew to operate winches and clutches.

Potential danger times are during three specific operations – tacking, gybing and reefing or unreefing the mainsail. Crew who are not involved should keep clear and move into the companionway.

Keep well clear of the falls (multiple lines) of the mainsheet, particularly if a track allows the mainsheet block to slide across the cockpit (as on the Sun Fast 37). On many cruising yachts, the mainsheet is secured to the coachroof just in front of the companionway. This opens up the cockpit and greatly reduces opportunity for accidents. The disadvantage is that more effort is required to pull the mainsheet in.

Cockpit lockers are usually beneath the seats on either side of the boat, and built into the transom containing the gas bottle for the galley. When opening lockers, always make sure that the heavy lids are securely held back. There is normally a short leash, which can be clipped to the nearest guardrail, preventing the lid from blowing back onto fingers, hands or your head!

The cockpit of this Oceanis 393 provides a protected area for the crew to sail in comfort and security, with direct access to the interior of the yacht.

2

TILLER OR WHEEL?

A smaller yacht will have a tiller, which is a straight (or slightly curved for comfort) lever connected directly to the head of the rudder. A larger yacht will have a wheel, indirectly connected to the rudder by steel wires and chain, geared systems or steel rods with optional hydraulic drive to lighten the load when turning the wheel.

A tiller is simple and straightforward with nothing to go wrong. There are two major disadvantages:

1. As yachts get bigger the steering gets heavier and it can become very tiring to keep sailing straight with a tiller.

2. The tiller takes up a lot of room in the cockpit, particularly when it sweeps across during tacks and gybes.

A wheel is mounted on a binnacle, which effectively divides the cockpit between helm and crew. The binnacle may be a multi-function pedestal fitted with the steering wheel, main steering compass, engine control lever and grab handle. It is a useful mounting position for electronic displays of information including speed and depth, plus electronic self-steering which is now standard on many cruising yachts. A large scale display for a chartplotter, displaying the GPS real time position and progress of the yacht,

The Hunter Horizon 232 is small enough to be perfectly balanced with transom-hung rudder and tiller.

can be mounted on the binnacle where it is perfectly positioned for the helm.

The larger the wheel, the less effort required to turn the rudder. However, a large wheel can make it difficult to get to the back of the boat, particularly when getting on or off at the transom. For this reason, some cruising yachts have twin wheels on either side at the stern, providing a clear passage from cockpit to transom. A wheel tends to be considerably less sensitive than a tiller – you get less feedback from the rudder when steering the boat. As you would expect, the most sensitive wheel systems tend to be expensive. Basic wheel systems can make it feel like you are steering through mush, but that can also be true of expensive hydraulics providing no feel at all. With a lot of different moving parts, wheel systems require maintenance and can fail. For that reason, all yachts with a wheel should be fitted with an emergency tiller system. This frequently looks like a crude iron bar, which lives at the bottom of a cockpit locker. It connects to the top of the rudder post aft of the binnacle and makes steering possible, but with very limited control.

Most yachts above 9 metres LOA (length overall) have wheel steering.

COACHROOF

When you walk on the coachroof, the raised area of deck on top of the main cabin area, beware that the non-slip area may not be as effective as on the side decks. It is also a wise precaution to close the sliding hatch above the companionway when anyone is moving around on the coachroof. Always beware of falling through open hatches, particularly late at night when you are stepping across yachts which have rafted up (moored alongside) in a crowded harbour. Try and avoid standing on the coachroof other than when you have to carry out a specific job. Move around the side decks where possible and remember to hold on!

The coachroof provides headroom in the main cabins as well as protection for the crew in the cockpit. The mast normally passes through a hole in the coachroof, protected by a waterproof gasket, with the mast foot secured above the keel.

CLEATS & FAIRLEADS

Most yachts have slots in the toerail known as fairleads on both sides of the bows and stern. Always lead mooring warps through these fairleads, which help to prevent ropes from chafing and ensure that stanchions do not get broken. Each fairlead has an adjacent horn cleat, normally two on the foredeck and one either side of the stern.

The 'horns' of this sophisticated cleat fold flat when not in use.

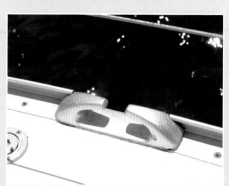

Fairlead set in the aluminium toerail on either side of the stern.

2

FOREDECK

When mooring or lowering and raising the anchor, one or two crew will need to move onto the foredeck. If your boat does not have a furling headsail, you need to hoist and drop sails on the foredeck. Most cruising boats these days have furling headsails, which greatly reduces the amount of work on the foredeck.

Protection from falling off the bows is provided by a stainless steel pulpit, encircling the foredeck. The pulpit is often fitted with port (red) and starboard (green) navigation lights and may have a step, so you can get ashore when moored bows-on to a dock.

A stainless steel pulpit.

An anchor locker.

On many cruising yachts, the anchor is stowed on the bow roller with the shank (straight arm of the anchor) secured horizontally. The chain is led through a hawse pipe into the anchor locker beneath the foredeck. When opening the lid of an anchor locker, always make sure it is held back. There is normally a leash, which attaches to the pulpit.

The advantage of this system is that the anchor is always ready for use and should be relatively easy to operate on the bow roller. If the anchor is stowed inside the anchor locker or on deck, it may be heavy and cumbersome to lift on and off the bow roller, particularly when fitted with chain.

Pulling chain out of the foredeck locker while preparing to drop anchor on a Bavaria 32. Note the pulpit has a step so crew can step ashore when moored bows-to a dock.

An electric anchor windlass.

An electric anchor windlass is recommended for cruising yachts longer than about 9 metres (29.5ft) LOA. This will remove most of the physical effort from hoisting or lowering the anchor with a large amount of heavy chain, which lays along the bottom and helps the anchor to hold. Remember to run your engine whilst using your anchor windlass to avoid flattening your batteries.

The foredeck of a cruising catamaran such as the Broadblue 38 provides unbeatable space for working or relaxing afloat.

The foredeck of the luxurious Nauticat 351 matches teak decking with teak guardrails as well as a teak platform over the bows.

SIDE DECKS

2

When a boat is under way, always hold on with at least one hand when moving along the side decks. Crouch low and use grab handles along each side of the coachroof. When the boat is heeling, it is preferable to move along the windward (uphill) side deck. If you are down to leeward, use the toerail (aluminium or teak capping above the join between hull and deck) as a foot brace. Always inform the helm before leaving the cockpit or moving along the side decks. Lines or webbing running down each side of the boat are called jackstays and are useful for clipping onto with your safety tether to ensure you don't fall overboard. Stainless steel stanchions complete with wire guardrails provide some further security when moving around the deck.

WATER & FUEL CAPS

Look out for circular steel water and fuel caps set into the deck. Both are clearly marked and it is vital to know which is which! A hexagonal key, normally stored in the chart table, or the end of a winch handle is used to unscrew each cap.

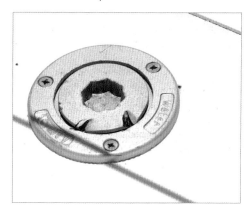

SHOES & BOOTS

On a boat you need shoes that have a good (limpet) grip, especially when moving around a glass fibre deck or coachroof when wet and slippery. Deck shoes are designed to grip without scratching the boat and there are many different styles available. Steer clear of cheap copies of well-known brands; the materials used and fit are usually poor. The following will help you understand the most common types and when to use them.

■ Leather moccasin style – extremely popular and comfortable to wear with lots of colours to choose from.

■ Trainer style – popular among younger boaters but beware of breathability problems if not made from leather.

■ Hybrid style – a cross-over between a shoe and a sandal, surprisingly comfortable, cheap to buy and great in warmer weather.

■ Sailing boots – if it's wet and cold you need sailing boots to move out of the cosy cockpit! Traditional rubber sailing boots work perfectly well and although leather boots may look stylish they are considerably more expensive.

Always avoid wearing deck shoes on shore. The soft soles necessary to grip the deck will wear out rapidly and dirt and grit picked up can scratch the boat's surface.

3 THE RIG

The rig provides power to drive the boat, with a series of controls to manage the sails in all conditions.

3

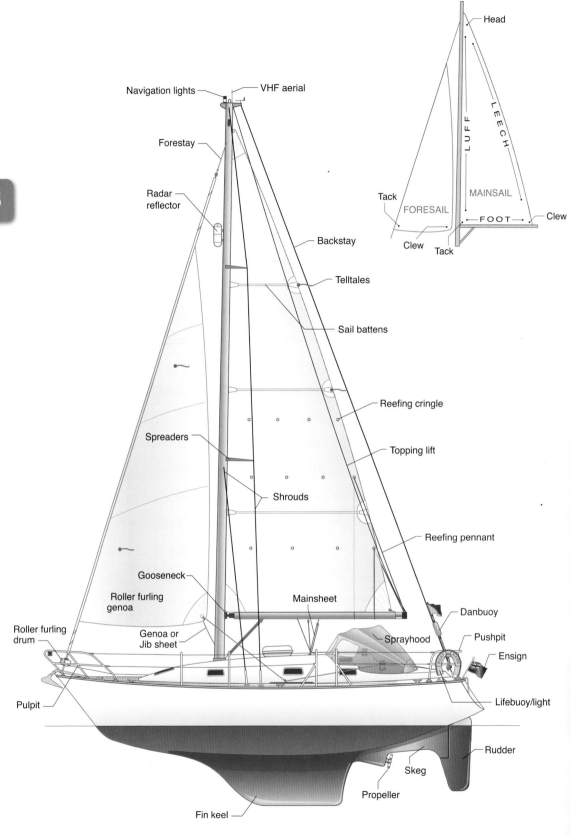

Navigation lights — VHF aerial

Forestay

Radar reflector

Backstay

Telltales

Sail battens

Reefing cringle

Spreaders

Topping lift

Shrouds

Reefing pennant

Gooseneck

Roller furling genoa

Mainsheet

Danbuoy

Roller furling drum

Genoa or Jib sheet

Sprayhood

Pushpit

Ensign

Pulpit

Lifebuoy/light

Rudder

Skeg

Propeller

Fin keel

Head

LUFF

LEECH

Tack

MAINSAIL

FORESAIL

FOOT

Clew

Clew

Tack

MAST & BOOM

Virtually all modern yachts have sloop rigs developed from the Bermuda Sloops of the 17th century, with a single mast and boom. A yawl has an additional mizzen mast aft of the main mast. A ketch has the mizzen ahead of the rudder but this style of rig has become rare.

Most cruising yachts are fitted with extruded aluminium masts and booms. You may see heavy wooden masts on classic yachts and lightweight carbon masts on high performance yachts, complete with a high performance price tag! The mast is supported by shrouds at the sides, a forestay at the bows and a backstay at the stern, all of which are commonly made with twisted stainless steel wires. Solid steel rod rigging may be found on more expensive yachts, while man-made materials such as Spectra® may be used for rigging on racing yachts, with the advantages of light weight, low drag and minimal stretch.

The forestay connects the stem of the yacht to the mast. If connected at the top of the mast, the yacht has a masthead rig. If connected further down the mast, the yacht has a fractional rig which might be at 7/8th or 3/4th of the mast height. An advantage of a fractional rig is that it allows greater control of mast bend, which can help to optimise the shape of the mainsail. If the

The Hunter Horizon 232 has a simple rig with single spreaders and modest sail area powering the 23 foot hull.

The Maestro 40R has a sophisticated rig with the mast supported by twin spreaders and a beautiful match between mainsail and high aspect jib.

yacht has an adjustable backstay, increased tension will bend the mast and tension the forestay, providing the headsail with a more efficient leading edge. When cruising, a more important benefit of a fractional rig is that smaller headsails are easier for the crew to manage, particularly when tacking.

The mast may have one or two sets of spreaders, which spread the load and prevent the mast bending sideways. In addition to the main shrouds, wire lowers help to support the middle of the mast.

MAINSAILS

Most cruising yachts have mainsails and headsails made of Dacron® which provides a good compromise between stretch, weight, durability and cost. Lightweight racing sails built of plastic laminate materials may have far superior weight and stretch characteristics to provide optimum performance, at greater cost with a shorter working life.

The mainsail is attached to the mast by the luff and to the boom by the foot, with the leech supported by stiff battens to help maintain the shape. Sail angle is controlled by a multi-purchase rope mainsheet. The size of the mainsail can be reduced by reefing as the wind increases. Slab reefing is the most popular method.

A parallel slab of sail is pulled down onto the boom, reducing the length of the luff and leech to reduce the size of the triangle. In-mast roller reefing is an alternative method, with the mainsail rolling up inside the mast. This looks neat, but the big disadvantage is that sail shape becomes progressively less efficient as size is reduced.

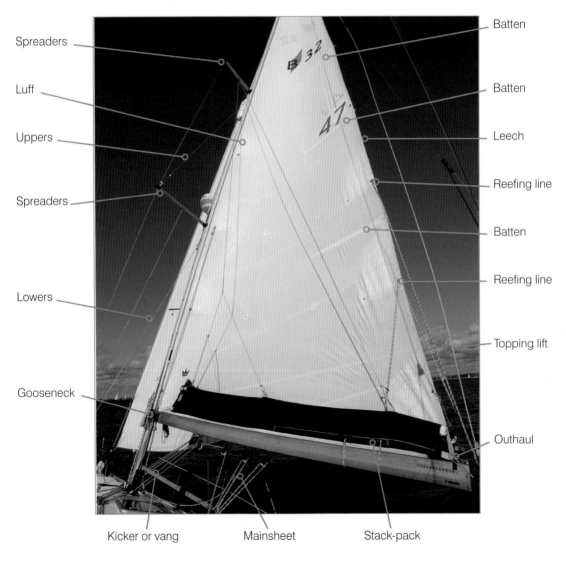

Spreaders — Luff — Uppers — Spreaders — Lowers — Gooseneck — Kicker or vang — Mainsheet — Stack-pack — Batten — Batten — Leech — Reefing line — Batten — Reefing line — Topping lift — Outhaul

HEADSAILS

The headsail is attached to the forestay by the luff, with the leech and foot unsupported. Sail angle is controlled by a rope sheet on each side of the boat, with the ends tied to the clew of the sail.

■ **Genoa** – A headsail that overlaps the mast when sailing upwind. The extra size of a genoa increases power, particularly on a reach, but it can be hard work pulling the sail flat when sailing upwind.

■ **Jib** – A headsail that does not overlap the mast. While there is less area and power than a genoa, a high aspect jib with a tall and narrow outline is highly efficient upwind, as well as being easy to handle. Loss of performance off the wind can be offset by use of a cruising chute or spinnaker.

■ **Furling headsail** – Most modern cruising yachts now have a furling headsail, which can be rolled away when moored or partly rolled to reduce the size of the headsail when sailing in stronger winds.

The **Broadblue 38 catamaran** has a lot of headsail power, with genoa overlapping the headsail and an even larger reacher (furled in the photo) for sailing offwind.

The headsail luff fits into a groove in an aluminium head-foil, which rotates around the forestay, using a halyard swivel above the head and furling drum below the tack. The drum is loaded with a furling line led back along the side deck. Let it off to unfurl the sail, which will wind the line onto the drum. Pull it in to furl the sail, which will unwind the line from around the drum. The headsail is generally left on the head-foil throughout the sailing season, although the rolled sail will slowly deteriorate through exposure to UV.

Furling headsails are designed to be as easy to operate as possible. They have one big disadvantage, which is a particular problem with large genoas. The shape of the sail will tend to get progressively fuller when you start to furl the sail for use in stronger winds. This means the boat will not be able to point as high into the wind.

The solution for optimum headsail performance is to only use a full size sail. Traditional cruising yachts may have three or more different sized headsails for different wind conditions. The headsail luff may be secured to the forestay by hanks – normally brass pistons – allowing each sail to be changed fairly quickly and easily. The main disadvantage is that changing down to a smaller size headsail may require the crew to work on the foredeck in difficult conditions, possibly with waves breaking over the pitching and rolling yacht. An additional disadvantage is that space (normally in the forepeak) will be required to stow all the headsails.

CRUISING CHUTES & SPINNAKERS

When the wind is blowing from behind the boat, a cruising chute or spinnaker will boost performance, giving a lot more sail area for running or broad reaching downwind. These sails are blown out like puffed-up cheeks. They are made of lightweight ripstop nylon, which is vulnerable to clumsy handling in a fresh breeze.

CRUISING CHUTE

A cruising chute has an asymmetric triangular profile with a full shape. The head is hoisted to the top of the forestay and the tack is secured by a strop to the stem of the yacht, with windward and leeward sheets led from the clew back to either side of the cockpit. Unlike a genoa, the luff is not attached to the forestay and sets in a smooth curve.

> A cruising chute is most effective on a broad reach, when the wind is blowing across the stern.

SPINNAKER

A spinnaker has a symmetric triangular profile with a very full shape. The head is hoisted to the top of the forestay. Unlike a cruising chute the tack and clew both float at the same height above the deck. On the windward side, the tack is held out by a spinnaker pole with a rope guy to adjust its horizontal angle, plus uphaul/downhaul ropes to control vertical angle. On the leeward side, the clew is controlled by a rope sheet. Unlike a genoa, the luff is not attached to the forestay and sets in a smooth curve. A spinnaker is very effective when the wind is blowing directly behind the boat, and can be used on a broad reach. The big disadvantage is that a spinnaker is considerably more complex and demanding than a cruising chute.

SAIL CONTROLS

WINCHES

Winches are used to pull in ropes by providing mechanical advantage when loads are too great for it to be possible or safe to do so by hand. A winch provides the power of a cart horse or tug-of-war team!

Halyard and sheet winches often have two speeds.

- Wind clockwise for high gear to pull as much rope as possible while the load is relatively light.
- Wind anti-clockwise for low gear to pull slowly when the load becomes heavy.

Cruising yachts are mainly fitted with self-tailing winches. The rope is held by jaws on top of the winch as you wind it in, allowing one person to operate a winch. If there are no self-tailing jaws, the rope must be pulled in by hand as you wind in, which requires two crew. Remember always to put three turns clockwise around the winch before taking up any load on the line.

On a medium-size cruising yacht, winches are likely to be used for the following main functions:

■ **Winding in and holding headsail sheets.** This requires the two most powerful primary winches on the boat, sited on the port and starboard side of the cockpit. These winches may also be used to control a spinnaker or cruising chute, when sailing downwind with the headsail furled.

■ **Winding up and tensioning the mainsail.** The load on the main halyard increases as the sail slides up the mast. It becomes necessary to use a smaller secondary winch to wind up the halyard and get the head right to the top. Secondary winches are normally mounted on the coachroof, either side of the companionway. They are also used for winding down reefing lines, when putting a reef in the mainsail.

3

WINCH HANDLES

■ Always remove handles from winches when not in use and make sure they are securely stowed inside the cockpit – two plastic sheaths are usually provided on either side of the companionway.

■ Winch handles can be heavy and quite cumbersome. Take care not to hit a fellow crew member as you move around the cockpit, particularly if the boat is moving around.

■ Be very careful not to let the handle fall over the side – it won't float!

The winch handle fits into the top of the winch. It can be wound clockwise, as well as anti-clockwise if the winch has two speeds.

WORKING WITH WINCHES

■ Winches invariably rotate in a clockwise direction. Anti-clockwise winches are occasionally used for specialist applications. When taking turns round the drum of the winch, keep your thumb and fingers on the outside as shown in fig. 1. Never let fingers or thumbs get between the rope and the drum.

■ Pull in slack on the rope and take enough turns round the drum to hold the load. Three turns should suffice for most uses on a small or medium size cruising yacht. If you put on too few turns, the rope will slip round the drum as soon as there is heavy load. If you put on too many turns, the turns will tend to ride up and overlap as you pull in the rope. This can create a 'riding turn' which locks the rope around the drum, with the result that it cannot be let off.

■ When you have pulled in three or more turns round the drum, lead the rope over the self-tailing feeder on top of the drum and pull it tight round the jaws with a final turn.

■ Insert the winch handle into the top of the drum and make sure it is fully down before you start winding. Some winch handles have a simple click-lock to ensure the handle cannot come out of the winch. If you are using a 2-speed winch, wind in high gear (clockwise) to start and then in low gear (anti-clockwise) when the load gets heavy.

■ When you have finished winding, unlock the handle and put it securely in the winch pocket by the companionway.

HOW TO LET OFF A RIDING TURN

If you put on too many turns before pulling in slack rope hand-over-hand, the turns tend to ride up and overlap. This is most likely to happen when the boat tacks and you are pulling in the new headsail sheet quickly. As soon as the headsail starts to load up and pull against the winch, any overlapping turns will lock inside turns against the drum. It is amazing to find that the rope has locked solid in a few seconds! To get out of this problem, you will need to take all the load off the winch. For instance, attach a second sheet to the headsail and pull it in on another winch until it takes all the load off the original sheet.

3

1 Lead the rope clockwise round the winch with your fingers and thumbs on the outside.

2 Take 3 or 4 turns round the drum so that the rope will hold without slipping.

3 Lead the rope over the stainless steel guide attached to the top of the winch.

4 Pull the rope tightly round the jaws, which will lock it in position.

3

CLUTCHES

Clutches enable the crew to use a variety of control lines with the fewest possible winches. For instance, in fig.1, six control lines led through six clutches can be served by a single winch, with five of the lines locked whilst one is operational. Having the fewest possible winches means considerably less cost, clutter and weight.

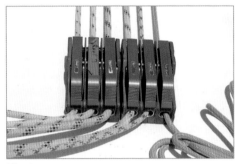

Fig. 1

Clutches are typically positioned either side of the companionway on the coachroof and are used for control lines led back from the base of the mast.

Typical uses will include:

■ **Main halyard** to pull the mainsail up to the top of the mast.

■ **Kicking strap** (boom vang). Control line for vertical angle of main boom, which needs to be eased off when pulling up the mainsail or reefing.

■ **Reefing lines** (pennants) for mainsail. Normally three colour-coded lines are used to pull down 1st, 2nd and 3rd reefs. Some yachts have double sets of reefing lines for the leech and luff led through clutches on either side of the companionway.

■ **Spinnaker halyard** to pull up a spinnaker or cruising chute; spinnaker pole uphaul and downhaul; control lines for vertical angle of spinnaker pole.

■ **Headsail halyard** to pull up a genoa or jib. If boat is equipped with furling headsail, this halyard is always locked with the sail fully hoisted. Apart from changing to a storm sail for extreme conditions, the halyard is only likely to be lowered for sail repairs or laying-up at the end of the season.

OPERATING CLUTCHES

1. When the clutch is closed (down) the rope can be pulled back (by pulling with your hands or winding with a winch) but cannot move forwards.

2. When the clutch is open (up) the rope will run free in either direction.

3. To lock the clutch, push the lever down.

4. To open the clutch, pull the lever up to the vertical position. If the rope is under tension, it may be difficult or impossible to lift the lever. The solution is to lead the rope around the winch and wind it back a couple of centimetres. This will take pressure off the clutch and enable you to lift the lever, before easing the rope from the winch.

TURNING BLOCKS

Halyards, reefing pennants, spinnaker pole uphaul and kicking strap control line are all led down to turning blocks on the coachroof. From there, they are led back to clutches on both sides of the coachroof, so they can be controlled from the cockpit.

3

HEADSAIL TRACK

Each port or starboard headsail sheet is led through a block on the side decks or coachroof, and back to a primary winch on the side of the cockpit. The block can be locked in different positions on its aluminium track.

■ Moving the block forward increases tension on the leech and reduces tension on the foot.

■ Moving the block back reduces tension on the leech and increases tension on the foot. This is necessary to keep leech and foot tension even when reducing the size of the headsail in stronger winds and for trimming for different points of sail.

Headsail sheet block   Headsail track

HEADSAIL FURLING LINE

The furling line which rolls the headsail is usually led back along the side deck to a turning block with a jammer just below the cockpit coaming. Let off the jammer to free the line when unrolling the headsail. The jammer works like a simple lever. It can be used to lock the furling line in any position when sailing with a partly furled headsail.

On this yacht the headsail furling line is led back along the coachroof, through the jammer and onto a winch.

3

MAINSHEET & TRAVELLER

The mainsheet controls the angle of the mainsail to the wind.

Most yachts have a multi-purchase mainsheet, with top and lower blocks typically providing a 6:1 purchase. This allows the mainsheet to be pulled in or let out by hand, without requiring a winch.

It is locked by a jamming cleat where the sheet exits the main block. Pull in and down to lock the sheet in the jaws of the cleat; pull in and up to unlock the sheet.

The lower block may be attached to a track, which allows it to be locked in different positions:

Centre – boom pulled in tight for beating to windward.

Port side – boom out near the shrouds for reaching or running on starboard tack.

Starboard side – boom out near the shrouds for reaching or running on port tack.

Off centre – useful to ease the boom away from the centreline if the yacht is overpowered when sailing to windward or on a fine reach.

If the traveller is inside the cockpit, it is a potential danger area. Keep well clear of the falls (bunch of ropes between the top and bottom blocks) of the mainsheet and traveller during tacks and gybes. When moving across an open traveller, always cross on the windward side which is clear of the mainsheet.

3

Most yachts have a multi-purchase mainsheet, with top and lower blocks typically providing a 6:1 purchase. This allows the mainsheet to be pulled in or let out by hand, without requiring a winch.

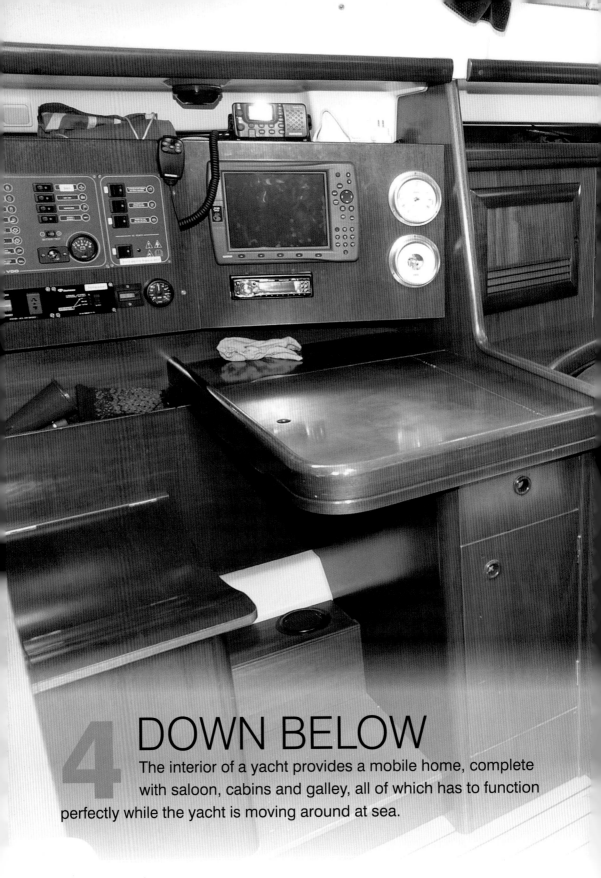

4 DOWN BELOW

The interior of a yacht provides a mobile home, complete with saloon, cabins and galley, all of which has to function perfectly while the yacht is moving around at sea.

STANDARD LAYOUT

Most yachts have a similar layout, which relies on a compromise between cruising comfort and performance under sail. A modern, medium size cruising yacht should provide two or three spacious double cabins, saloon area with sufficient table space for 6–8 people, spacious galley, one or two WC/shower cubicles and navigation/planning area, with large amounts of storage space and standing headroom throughout most of the interior.

THE COMPANIONWAY

4

The companionway is the main entrance to the interior. It is usually closed by a sliding horizontal hatch and a vertical washboard, which may be divided into two or three overlapping washboards. These hatches can, in good conditions, be left open while at sea, but are designed to provide a water-proof barrier if the yacht is caught in extreme conditions.

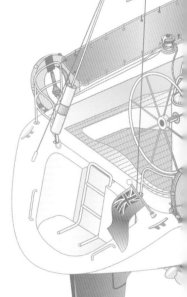

Companionway steps lead down to the floor of the saloon, which may be a significant distance below the cockpit, representing a significant hazard if you were to slip. When using the steps hold the grab handles on either side of the companionway. If the yacht is under way, it may be safer to descend facing backwards. Make sure the steps are securely locked in position. A grab bag with essentials for the liferaft should ideally be stowed near the top of the companionway ladder.

Bolt croppers and an axe are conveniently positioned near the companionway hatch.

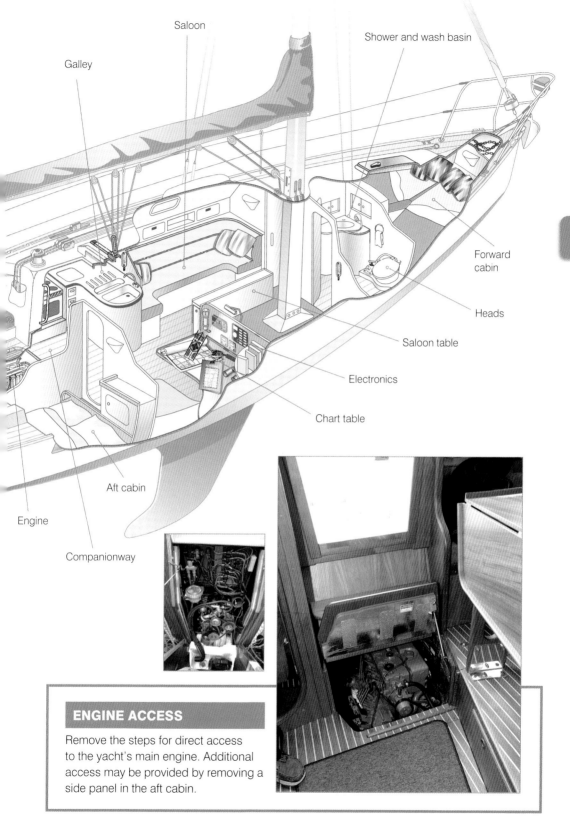

Saloon

Galley

Shower and wash basin

Forward cabin

Heads

Saloon table

Electronics

Chart table

Aft cabin

Engine

Companionway

4

ENGINE ACCESS

Remove the steps for direct access to the yacht's main engine. Additional access may be provided by removing a side panel in the aft cabin.

THE GALLEY

On board a boat the 'kitchen' is known as a galley. Here we look at some of the useful features you should find on board.

STOVE WITH DOUBLE BURNERS AND OVEN

The majority of yacht stoves 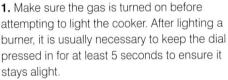(A) are fuelled by gas, which is efficient and economical. However, since gas is heavier than air, great care needs to be taken that it does not leak and possibly build up an explosive mixture under the floorboards. If there is a gas stop cock in the galley, it should always be closed when the cooker is not in use. The gas cylinder, usually kept in a cockpit locker near the stern, should ideally be turned off at the same time as the cooker.

1. Make sure the gas is turned on before attempting to light the cooker. After lighting a burner, it is usually necessary to keep the dial pressed in for at least 5 seconds to ensure it stays alight.

2. The boat may roll or pitch at sea. For security, a pan or kettle should be locked in position with metal fiddles. In addition, the stove is mounted on gimbals so it can swing as the boat heels.

3. Familiarise yourself with grab handles and brace points before using a cooker at sea. Avoid filling pans or kettles (B) more than half full to minimise the dangers from hot liquids.

Cooker on gimbals swings as the yacht heels.

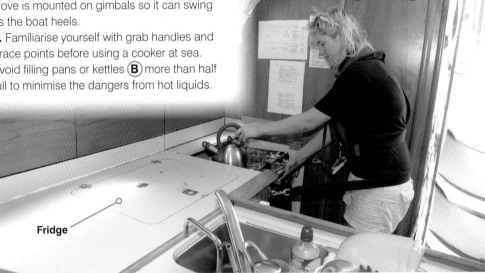

Fridge

Lean back against a safety strap if the yacht heels away from the cooker. When cooking whilst under way wear your foul weather gear trousers and fully enclosed shoes to avoid being burned if liquids splash from the cooker top.

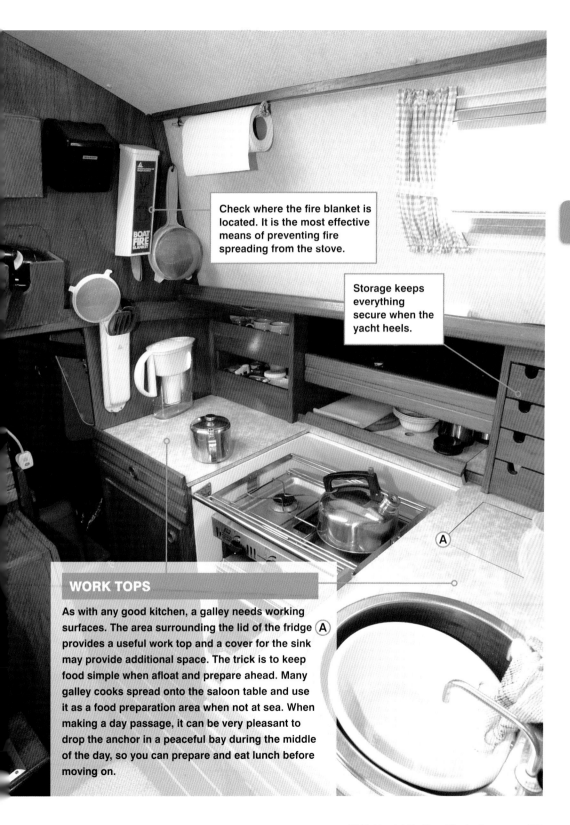

4

Check where the fire blanket is located. It is the most effective means of preventing fire spreading from the stove.

Storage keeps everything secure when the yacht heels.

Ⓐ

WORK TOPS

As with any good kitchen, a galley needs working surfaces. The area surrounding the lid of the fridge Ⓐ provides a useful work top and a cover for the sink may provide additional space. The trick is to keep food simple when afloat and prepare ahead. Many galley cooks spread onto the saloon table and use it as a food preparation area when not at sea. When making a day passage, it can be very pleasant to drop the anchor in a peaceful bay during the middle of the day, so you can prepare and eat lunch before moving on.

CHILLER/FRIDGE

Modern cruising yachts will have a large chiller/fridge underneath the work surface, with access via a heavy, insulated lid (A) that should be locked open while you are burrowing inside. A drain plug in the bottom is activated by an electric pump. Compartments provide plenty of storage space, but it is tricky to get everything in the right position. For instance, keep the most used items near the top of the compartment. Provisions must be secure enough not to roll with the yacht – broken eggs and squashed tomatoes can make a very nasty mess!

The main problem with yacht fridges is that they use a lot of electricity, okay when you can plug into shore power in a marina, but without shore power, your fridge will rapidly drain the batteries when not running the engine. This will not affect starting the engine, which should have a separate battery, but cabin lights may dim when the fridge ceases to function. Maintaining a cold fridge without shore power in a hot sailing area, such as the Mediterranean or Caribbean, could require at least 3–4 hours with the engine running divided between morning, afternoon and early evening. When the engine is off, make sure the fridge is turned off as well!

STORAGE

The galley has cupboards for crockery and drawers for cutlery etc. Make sure lockers and drawers are locked closed whenever the yacht gets under way, or you will have plates, knives, glassware (B) and forks flying all over the place.

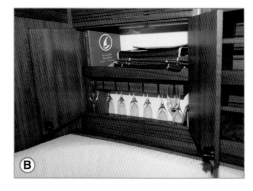

A trash cupboard under the sink can also be a useful space for cleaning materials. If there is too much trash, seal it in plastic bags and stow in the cockpit lockers with empty glass and plastic bottles until you go ashore. Always dispose of your trash with the utmost care and consideration for the people who live at local harbours and anchorages. Never throw anything over the side.

Pots and pans take up a lot of space and need to be stacked carefully. On some yachts, you may find them stowed under the saloon table (C) or inside a bench seat.

GALLEY SINK

A double sink is a big help for storing crockery and cups in a temporary safe location, especially if you need to wash-up when the yacht is under way. Most modern yachts have a pressurised water supply, with cold or hot water on tap, just like at home. There are three fundamental differences:

■ A yacht has limited water supply. It is wise to regularly fill the tanks and check the water levels – a gauge is usually in the chart table area.

■ Hot water may be provided by running the engine or plugging into shore power, although it can stay hot for a few hours after the engine has been turned off.

■ Pressurised water needs battery power which is charged by the engine, although taps can run without any engine for a surprisingly long time.

There may also be a foot pump. Check whether this supplies salt water, which was standard practice for washing up or cooking vegetables on board older cruising yachts.

When you fill up with water, check if the water is safe to drink. Apart from that, it may pick up the taste of the tanks and be unpalatable. You can flush out the tanks with a dedicated tank-cleaning product available from chandleries or sanitise the tanks with dissolving tablets such as Puriclean. Best advice is to carry a large supply of bottled water in plastic containers for drinking at the table.

4

THE SALOON

A yacht's saloon fulfils many functions; chart table, eating and sleeping area. When under way it is essential it is kept clear and anything that may become loose is stowed safely away and will not fall on the floor or roll around.

4

The standard layout is to have a large drop-flap table with comfortable settees on either side. If you don't mind crowding out the boat, (A) the settees can also be used as berths, with the option of lowering the table and putting in an extra cushion to form a double berth on one side. If you want to sleep in the saloon while the yacht is under way, a lee cloth will be required to prevent you rolling out of bed.

Most modern yachts have a shallow bilge under the saloon floor and sections of floor can be pulled up to check if the automatic bilge pump is working. It may also provide access to sea cocks and the log, which is used to measure the yacht's speed and can sometimes get clogged with weed.

FORECABIN

Light and airy thanks to the forehatch, the forecabin will usually have room for two berths, providing a comfortable double bed. (B) Headroom may be compromised if the forecabin extends beyond the coachroof and is not a good place for sleeping when the yacht is under way, as the bows will pitch up and down more than any other part of the yacht.

The double berth in the forecabin is recommended in harbour, but not when the yacht is pitching at sea!

The saloon of a cruising cat or 'pilot house' yacht provides great visibility and the highest levels of comfort at anchor.

The saloon can be a multipurpose venue for planning, socialising, eating or sleeping.

4

4

AFT CABINS

Modern cruising yachts tend to have very wide sterns, with the possible disadvantage of getting pushed around by waves in a following sea. The advantage is that you can fit in extra accommodation, with two double cabins or one very large double across the back of the boat. For yacht designers, the main problem is fitting the cabin or cabins under the cockpit sole, which will not allow standing headroom unless the yacht has a high-rise stern. The aft cabin can be a secure place to sleep when the yacht is under way, but you may get disturbed by action in the cockpit and it will be extremely noisy when the engine is running.

The luxurious aft cabin of a Nauticat 351 provides standing headroom and a settee next to a proper double bed.

HEADS

Heads is the yachtsman's term for a nautical WC, and on modern cruising yachts is normally a self-contained unit with lavatory, washbasin and shower. Larger yachts may have two or more, which are en-suite with cabins.

■ The sea cocks for the WC may need to be closed when the yacht is heeling with the heads on the leeward (downhill) side. Make sure you know where the levers are located.

■ The most popular style of WC operates on a pump system, which may be a hand pump or electric. Flick the switch to the pump position and pump seawater through the bowl. Then flick the switch to the dry position and pump most of the water out of the bowl.

SEA COCKS

Sea cocks are outlets or inlets in the hull, used to pump out waste or pump in seawater. The primary uses are:

▓ Seawater is pumped in and out through sea cocks to cool the engine.

Seawater is pumped in and out through sea cocks to flush the WC.

▓ Each sea cock will normally have a red lever, which turns open or shut through about 90°. Open is in line with the inlet or outlet pipe.

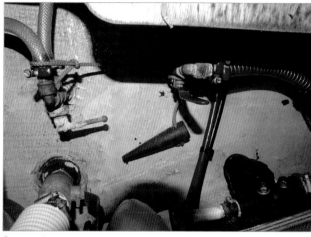

Sea cocks get corroded with age and in extreme cases may fail. A wooden bung can be hammered into the hole to prevent water from flooding into the hull.

▓ A marine WC has a narrow outlet pipe, which is easy to block. Some people believe you should not use toilet paper. My own experience is that there is no problem putting down a modest amount of thin toilet paper, so long as you pump it out with enthusiasm. If in doubt, keep pumping!

▓ In some countries holding tanks are a legal requirement. They are particularly desirable in tideless areas such as the Baltic and Mediterranean, and in my opinion should be fitted to all new yachts and used as a matter of course by all. The waste from the WC is diverted to the holding tank, which can be emptied far out at sea or at a special pumping station.

▓ The sink should have pressurised hot and cold water. It is usually possible to use the heads as a shower cubicle, using an electric pump to clear out the water. Be warned that it is not pleasant to see a lot of foamy detritus being pumped out when you are moored near other yachts, which may be illegal in a harbour or marina.

STOWING GEAR

Always take soft bags on yachts and keep your gear to a minimum. The forecabin and aft cabins may have lockers, side shelves and space under the berths. There may also be storage under the saloon berths, unless they are filled by lifejackets, batteries or water tanks. Additional cupboards and shelves may be behind the berths. You may be able to store empty bags under berths or in cockpit lockers. Alternatively, unpack and leave the bags ashore.

A wet locker is very useful for hanging up wet weather gear when not being used. The best location is adjacent to the companionway, so the warm air from the engine dries your soaking wet jacket and trousers, which can drip into the bilge.

Convenient space for long term storage under the forecabin berths on the Maestro 40R.

NAVIGATION ZONE

The chart table area, normally opposite the galley by the side of the companionway, is where all yacht's management is conducted – operating the electric switch panel, planning your passage, working out routes and plotting your position, checking forecasts, listening to the VHF radio or booking into a marina.

4

CHART TABLE

On a medium-sized yacht, this should be large enough to lay out a half-folded chart. Lift the lid and you will find the necessary charts for your cruising area, plus instruments to work with the chart: dividers to measure distance, a plastic plotter or parallel rules to show bearings, a soft pencil and rubber to annotate the chart, plus a notebook to record a passage plan. A log book is used to record each day's passage with information including times, position, bearings, sea state and wind strength. In some countries, it is a legal requirement to keep the log up to date. Prior to your trip check whether a licence or qualification is required for the area in which you will be sailing. The inside of the chart table is a useful place to stow essentials including a hand-bearing compass, hand-held GPS, the key to open diesel and water tank caps and your mobile phone, which can be useful afloat but should never be relied on. There should be a large folder containing the yacht manual and separate instructions for equipment such as VHF and GPS. Pilot guides (providing invaluable information on harbours, marinas and anchorages in your cruising area) and tide tables can be stowed by the side of the chart table.

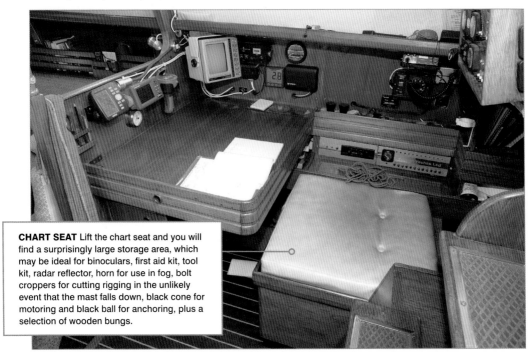

CHART SEAT Lift the chart seat and you will find a surprisingly large storage area, which may be ideal for binoculars, first aid kit, tool kit, radar reflector, horn for use in fog, bolt croppers for cutting rigging in the unlikely event that the mast falls down, black cone for motoring and black ball for anchoring, plus a selection of wooden bungs.

VHF RADIO

VHF radio provides communication between all craft, as well as marine emergency services such as the Coastguard and RNLI. Unlike a mobile phone, VHF does not rely on a land-based signal and can provide line of sight communication at sea up to a maximum distance of around 60 miles if communicating 'ship to shore' or around 25 miles if communicating 'ship to ship'. This presumes that the VHF aerials can see each other – VHF will not work if a land mass blocks the signal. VHF normally uses simplex transmission. You can talk or listen, but cannot do both at the same time. A hand-held VHF set provides useful back-up and can be used from any part of the yacht.

4

CHART TABLE AREA Rod Carr uses the port side of the saloon of his cruising catamaran as a dedicated navigation area with a chart table suitable for half-size charts and direct access to GPS, chartplotter, VHF radio and on-board computer.

4

OPERATING VHF

It is good practice to keep a radio watch by listening to Ch16 when under way.

Channel 16 is the international distress frequency for maritime use. It is used to broadcast three important safety messages:

1. **Mayday for grave and imminent danger requiring immediate assistance.**
2. **Pan Pan for an urgent safety message.**
3. **Securite for a navigational safety message.**

The Coastguard uses Ch16 to provide regular weather forecasts and warnings. Ch16 is also used to initiate contact with another yacht or vessel. As soon as contact is made, you must change to a different channel.

A yacht must be licensed for VHF radio. This licence provides a Maritime Mobile Service Identity (MMSI) number for use with Digital Selective Calling (DSC). This distress alert works in conjunction with the Global Maritime Distress and Safety System (GMDSS). Pressing the emergency button will activate DSC alarms on all radios within range and keep sending the yacht's MMSI number and position until DSC is deactivated. This DSC alarm should be followed by an oral Mayday transmission.

In the UK, any vessel operating with VHF must also have on board someone qualified to use the equipment. The RYA administers an SRC shore-based course, which is widely available.

Talking on VHF is not like using a phone. Think what you are going to say and make it clear who is sending the message, by repeating the name of your yacht three times. Remember to press the send button, speak slowly and clearly, then release the button while waiting for a response. If reception is poor, try turning the 'squelch' dial until the incoming voice is clear.

Never say "Over and out". It is nonsense! "Over" is when you wish to hear the other person speak and release the send button; "Out" is when you are ending your transmission.

VHF PHONETICS

The phonetic alphabet can make it much easier to understand a VHF message. For instance if you call up a marina to request a berth for your yacht 'Uno', spell it out – Uniform-November-Oscar. To make it easy, keep a list of phonetic letters next to the VHF radio:

A Alpha	J Juliet	S Sierra
B Bravo	K Kilo	T Tango
C Charlie	L Lima	U Uniform
D Delta	M Mike	V Victor
E Echo	N November	W Whiskey
F Foxtrot	O Oscar	X X-ray
G Golf	P Papa	Y Yankee
H Hotel	Q Quebec	Z Zulu
I India	R Romeo	

RYA VHF PUBLICATIONS

A selection of RYA publications to help you get the most from your VHF radio.

EMERGENCY MESSAGES

MAYDAY

A Mayday message is sent on Ch16. Remember that Mayday must only be used when there is grave and imminent danger requiring immediate assistance. For instance, if a crew member is critically injured or the yacht is in imminent danger of sinking. It is a wise precaution to keep a Mayday crib close to the VHF radio, along the lines of:

- Mayday, Mayday, Mayday
- This is yacht Uno, Uno, Uno
- Call sign and MMSI number
- Mayday yacht Uno
- Call sign and MMSI number
- Position 50 degrees, 38 minutes, 20 seconds North, 1 degree, 42 minutes, 10 seconds West.
- Yacht on fire and sinking fast.
- We require immediate assistance.
- Seven crew on board.
- Over.

PAN PAN

Do not send a Mayday when Pan Pan will suffice for an urgent message on Ch16, along the lines of:

- Pan Pan, Pan Pan, Pan Pan
- This is yacht Uno, Uno, Uno
- Call sign and MMSI number
- Pan Pan yacht Uno
- Call sign and MMSI number
- Position 50 degrees, 38 minutes, 20 seconds North, 1 degree, 42 minutes, 10 seconds West.
- We are dismasted and require assistance.
- Seven crew on board.
- Over.

GPS

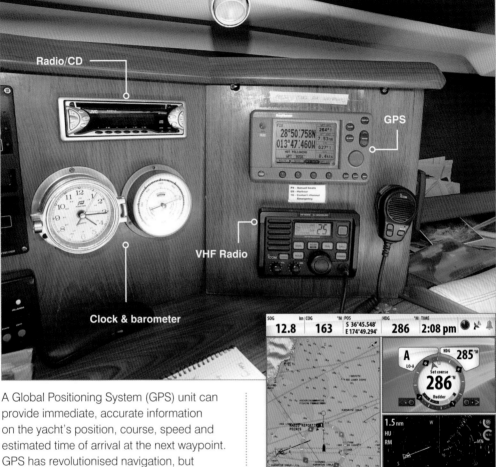

Radio/CD

GPS

VHF Radio

Clock & barometer

A sophisticated Multi Function Display

A Global Positioning System (GPS) unit can provide immediate, accurate information on the yacht's position, course, speed and estimated time of arrival at the next waypoint. GPS has revolutionised navigation, but should always be used with full back-up by traditional paper chart navigation – satellite signals or electric supply can suddenly fail!

A chartplotter combines electronic charts with GPS. This enables you to follow the real-time progress of your yacht across a chart on a colour screen. As with a basic GPS unit, a chartplotter provides immediate information on the yacht's position, course, speed and estimated time of arrival at the next waypoint. It also allows you to 'Find Yacht' at any time, check exactly where you are on the chart and access immediate information on nearby dangers such as underwater rocks. A more sophisticated Multi Function Display can combine chartplotter with radar,

depth sounder, AIS (Automatic Identification System), engine information and general entertainment. Always cross-check your GPS position using a secondary means of position fixing.

RADIO/CD

Useful for weather forecasts as well as relaxation. Keep the volume down when there are other yachts around, particularly if there are speakers in the cockpit!

Main switch panel

Gas alarm

4

CLOCK & BAROMETER

Traditional instruments for the navigator. Use the barometer to check barometric pressure. In simple terms, going up indicates fair weather and going down may be heading towards foul weather, particularly if there is a big drop in pressure.

MAIN SWITCH PANEL

A cruising yacht will have two or more batteries for general electrical requirements and one battery dedicated to starting the engine. You will normally find the principal battery switches – red plastic levers that turn through 90 degrees – behind the chart table area or companionway steps. When the yacht is occupied, you will normally leave all the battery switches on.

The main switch panel is used to turn on individual switches for uses such as cabin lights, navigation lights, anchor light, pressurised water, automatic bilge pump, VHF, GPS, cockpit instruments including boat speed, depth sounder and autopilot. It may also display the state of battery charging and current water and fuel levels.

GAS ALARM

The gas alarm will indicate if you have a gas leak. Keep it turned on.

READ A BOOK

RYA Electrics Handbook (E-G67) by Andrew Simpson

Chapters include basic theory of electricity, different types of batteries, engine start systems, circuit protection and monitoring, engine charging and primary circuits.

5 THE SAFETY BRIEFING

When the crew are new to a yacht, they should be given a comprehensive safety and equipment briefing before leaving the dock. This is a typical 'tick list' for a briefing on a medium-sized yacht.

SALOON AND FORECABIN

- Location and use of fire extinguishers and fire blanket for galley.
- Safe operation of cooker and gas.
- Always secure the lid of the fridge when open.
- Only run the fridge with shore or engine power.
- Stow gear carefully so it will not move with the yacht. Make sure all cupboards and drawers are locked shut.
- Close hatches and ports in the foredeck and coachroof. Indicate emergency exits via hatches.
- Explain how pressurised hot and cold water is provided. Make clear that only limited amounts are available.
- Demonstrate engine access and necessary checks such as oil level.
- Demonstrate how to extinguish an engine fire by firing foam through the 'fire hole' without opening up the engine and letting in air.
- Show how to open and close sea cocks for the engine. Locate and explain how to use wooden bungs if a sea cock fails.
- Demonstrate how to switch on/off individual batteries.
- Point out and explain use of anchor windlass overload switch.

Extinguisher and blanket – fire could be devastating on a yacht.

Stop cocks are located under the floorboards and in the heads and galley.

Check that bilge pump hoses are functional.

DON'T GET BURNT! Learn how to use the galley safely and turn off the gas. When cooking at sea wear foul weather trousers and closed shoes to avoid serious burns.

CHART TABLE AREA

Explain and demonstrate how to use:
- Main electric switch panel.
- VHF radio including Ch16, DSC, Mayday and Pan-Pan procedures.
- GPS unit including multi-function display if fitted.
- Check water tank levels.
- Check gas detector and low battery alarm.
- Locate hand-held VHF and emergency VHF aerial (used if the main aerial on the mast fails).
- Locate and work through the First Aid box.
- Locate and work through tool box.
- Locate flares and grab bag for liferaft.
- Explain any other equipment stored in navigator's seat such as motoring cones, mooring balls, bolt croppers and foghorn.

Watertight storage for flares and other safety gear.

5

Do you know how to use a First Aid Kit? Take a course!

A black ball goes up when the anchor goes down.

Time to blow your trumpet – there may be fog!

AFT CABINS

- Location and use of fire extinguishers.
- Make sure hatches and ports are tightly closed for use at sea. A larger yacht may have an emergency exit in the cockpit or stern.

HEADS

- Demonstrate how the WC functions. Make clear that misuse can cause blockages, which the 'blocker' has to clear!
- Explain about the shower pump.

COCKPIT & DECK

Horseshoe buoy and danbuoy are for man overboard.

Flares have different uses – get the right one for light or dark conditions.

5

Learn how to use a throwing line.

■ Demonstrate how to use flares and explain expiry dates.

■ Explain how to use flares safely to attract the attention of a helicopter and the use of an earthing line.

■ Demonstrate how to put on and adjust a lifejacket – check light and CO_2 inflation.

■ Demonstrate how to put on and adjust a harness – identify where to clip on in the cockpit and on deck.

■ Explain how the liferaft is prepared for use – remember to attach it to the yacht before chucking over the side!

■ Locate the emergency tiller and attach to rudder post.

■ Explain the use of dan and horseshoe buoys, drogue and lights, all of which are stowed on the pushpit.

■ Demonstrate how to throw a coiled rope and a weighted throwing line.

■ Demonstrate safe use of winches and handles.

■ Demonstrate safe use of sheet traveller and mainsheet. This is particularly important when they are inside the cockpit.

■ Explain how to gybe safely – potentially the most dangerous manoeuvre under sail.

5

Emergency tiller if the wheel fails.

Mains electricity connection.

Tight turns are essential when furling the headsail around the forestay.

Ropes, cleats and winches can be dangerous if you don't understand them.

6 WIND STRENGTH

The Beaufort Scale is the yachtsman's favourite measure of wind strength, which can also be represented as knots when recording true or apparent wind.

THE BEAUFORT WIND SCALE

Admiral Sir Francis Beaufort, who lived from 1774–1857, is credited with the invention of the Beaufort Scale in 1806 while serving on board HMS *Woolwich*. In times long before reliable anemometers, it was used to help sailors estimate wind strength by matching the appearance of the open sea against a list of careful descriptions. It seems likely that similar scales of wind force were in use many years before Admiral Beaufort was even born, but the immortal Admiral still gets all the credit! In modern times, the Beaufort Scale is still widely used for maritime weather forecasts and quoted by yachtsmen as the official gauge of the wind.

Force 4 provides perfect yacht sailing conditions for a traditional yacht – neither too little nor too much wind!

Force	Knots	Mph	km/h	Description
0	0–1	0	0	**Calm**

On land: Smoke rises vertically.
At sea: Like a mirror.
Typical conditions: No use for sailing. Either stay in the marina or turn on the engine.

1	1–3	1–3	1–6	**Light air**

On land: Wind direction indicated by smoke drift.
At sea: Ripples on the water without foam crests.
Typical conditions: Still not enough wind for sailing – a yacht will barely move.

2	4–6	4–7	7–11	**Light breeze**

On land: Wind felt on face and leaves begin to rustle.
At sea: Small wavelets but crests do not break.
Typical conditions: The yacht will pick up a little speed under sail and may heel slightly, giving a balanced feel to steering. Progress is likely to be very slow if you sail directly downwind.

3	7–10	8–12	12–19	**Gentle breeze**

On land: Wind extends light flags. Leaves and twigs in constant motion.
At sea: Large wavelets with a few white horses.
Typical conditions: The start of a good sailing breeze. The yacht will start to perform well on all points under full sail.

WHAT ARE KNOTS? 1 knot = 1 nautical mile per hour. A few hundred years before the appearance of GPS, sailors tied knots in a rope and trailed it behind to assess the speed of their ship. 1 nautical mile = 1.15 statute miles = 1,852 metres.
1 nautical mile corresponds to 1 minute of latitude.

Force	Knots	Mph	km/h	Description
4	11–16	13–18	20–29	Moderate breeze

On land: Dust and loose paper raised. Small branches are moved.
At sea: Small waves with fairly frequent white horses.
Typical conditions: Perfect conditions for sailing on a reach. Upwind the bows may start pitching in waves. Downwind the yacht may start rolling – the solution is to head up onto a broad reach. If the yacht starts heeling past 30 degrees, it is time to reduce sail by partly furling the headsail and taking one reef in the mainsail. If the wind gets stronger, all the crew are advised to wear lifejackets and be prepared to clip on with harnesses.

Force	Knots	Mph	km/h	Description
5	17–21	19–24	30–39	Fresh Breeze

On land: Smaller trees sway.
At sea: Moderate waves with many white horses.
Typical conditions: Good sailing conditions if you are experienced, but the sea may become rough and uncomfortable. Reduce sail to keep the boat under full control. Making progress upwind may become slow and difficult. Consider heading for shelter as soon as possible.

Force	Knots	Mph	km/h	Description
6	22–27	25–31	40–50	Strong Breeze

On land: Large branches are swaying. Umbrellas are used with difficulty.
At sea: Large waves start to form with white foam crests and some spray.
Typical conditions: Your comfort level will depend on personal experience and sea conditions, which may become particularly unpleasant in areas of shallow water. Making progress upwind could require help from the engine – even then it may be painfully slow. All sensible yachtsmen will be tucked up in a safe anchorage or marina.

Force	Knots	Mph	km/h	Description
7	28–33	32–38	51–62	Near Gale

On land: Inconvenience felt when walking against the wind with whole trees swaying around.
At sea: Sea heaps up with white foam blown in streaks along the waves.
Typical conditions: Yachts should seek shelter, taking great care on the final approach to an anchorage or marina.

Force	Knots	Mph	km/h	Description
8	34–40	39–46	63–74	Gale

On land: Twigs break off trees.
At sea: Wave crests break into spindrift.
Typical conditions: Experienced sailors will stay offshore – conditions may be more dangerous close to land. Maximum reefs in mainsail and headsail. It may be preferable to heave-to and ride out the storm.

Force	Knots	Mph	km/h	Description
9	41–47	47–54	75–88	Severe Gale

On land: Roof and fence damage.
At sea: Sea heaps up with white foam blown in streaks along the waves.
Typical conditions: Riding out the storm under storm sails.

Force	Knots	Mph	km/h	Description
10–12	48–64+	55–73+	89–118+	Storm to Hurricane

On land: Trees uprooted and structural damage.
At sea: Very high waves with overhanging crests. Sea covered in white foam.
Typical conditions: Riding out the storm under 'bare poles' with possible use of sea anchor.

TRUE WIND & APPARENT WIND

True wind is the wind speed and direction blowing onto a stationary object, such as a stationary yacht in a marina.

Apparent wind is wind speed and direction experienced by a moving object, such as a yacht under sail or power.

Apparent wind is directly linked to a yacht's course. If you sail (or motor) towards the true wind direction, apparent wind will increase. If you sail (or motor) away from the true wind direction, apparent wind will decrease. For instance, if your boat is moving through the water at 5 knots in a true wind of 15 knots, apparent wind would decrease to 10 knots on a course directly away from the wind, or increase to 20 knots on a course directly towards the wind. This explains why beating upwind can feel a lot colder and rougher that running downwind in the

Sailing towards the wind effectively increases apparent wind and puts greater pressure on the sails.

same true wind speed. It is easy to get caught out by this phenomenon. If you are enjoying a lovely broad reach, check for following white horses before you change course onto a beat, which may become a nasty wet ride.

Sailing away from the wind effectively reduces apparent wind and puts less pressure on the sails.

Apparent wind is wind speed and direction experienced by a moving object, such as a yacht under sail or power.

7 THE GOOD KNOT GUIDE

Knots play a vital role in sailing. They are used to secure ropes and must be completely reliable. Plenty of practice will ensure that six of the most useful knots can always be tied correctly.

TYPES OF KNOT

BEND – knot that ties two ropes together. **HITCH** – knot that ties rope to a ring or post.

ROUND TURN AND TWO HALF HITCHES

- Good multi-purpose knot that can be untied under tension.
- Typical uses include attaching dinghy painter or mooring line to a ring. Can also be used for securing fenders.

REEF KNOT

- Traditional knot used to tie reefs into the mainsail. However, 'reefing points' (short lines attached to the mainsail) are seldom used on modern cruising yachts. A reef knot will only work properly with ropes or lines of the same diameter.

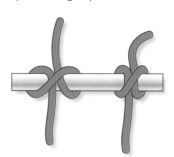

CLOVE HITCH

- Quick to tie and easy to adjust.
- Typical uses include attaching fenders to guardrails.

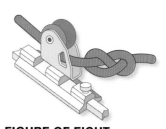

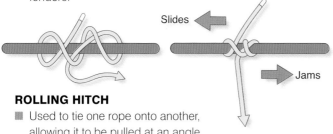

Slides

Jams

ROLLING HITCH

- Used to tie one rope onto another, allowing it to be pulled at an angle.
- Typical use could include taking the load off a jib sheet in order to clear a riding turn.

FIGURE-OF-EIGHT

- Used to tie a stopper knot in the end of a rope.
- Typical uses include putting a figure-of-eight in the end of headsail sheets, to prevent them pulling out of the block.

7

PARTS OF A ROPE

Working End – end of the rope (or line) that you use to make the knot.

Working Part – rope between the working end and knot.

Standing End – end of the rope that is not being used for the knot.

Standing Part – rope between the standing end and knot.

Bitter End – end of the rope that is tied off or secured to a fixed object.

Bight – curved or U-shaped part of the rope.

Loop – a rope circle formed by the working end.

Elbow – the working end crosses the rope twice, as in a figure-of-eight.

Turns – single turn is once over, round turn is twice over, two round turns is three times over.

HOW TO TIE A SHEET BEND

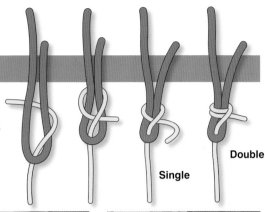

Single

Double

- Used to tie two ropes together. Most effective if ropes are of different diameter. A double sheet bend provides extra security.
- Typical uses could include tying two ropes together to provide sufficient length when attaching a stern line to a tree or rock on the shore.

7

1 Start the sheet bend with a loop in the end of the bigger rope and pull the thinner end through.

2 Lead the thinner end round the back of the loop and down to cross under itself.

3 Pull tight. For extra security, take two turns round the back of the loop.

HOW TO TIE A BOWLINE

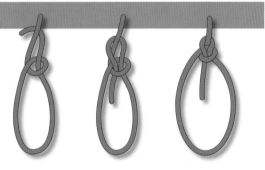

- Used to tie a loop in the end of a rope. Quick to tie and very secure, but cannot be untied when the rope is under tension. It must be slackened off to untie the bowline.
- Typical uses include mooring and attaching sheets to a headsail.

1 Pull the working end up through a loop in the working part of the rope.

2 Lead the working end round the back of the standing part and down through the loop.

3 Pull the bowline tight. The knot will not slip, but will come undone when required.

SECURING A ROPE TO A CLEAT

Always start by taking one turn round the base of the cleat, followed by a series of figure-of-eight turns and a final round turn for maximum friction.

READ A BOOK

RYA Knots, Splices & Ropework Handbook (G63)
by Gordon Perry and Steve Judkins

Complete guide to knots including rope construction and maintenance, basic knots essential for boating activities, blocks and tackles, lashing and bindings, splicings and decorative knots.

RYA Pocket Guide to Boating Knots (G60)
All the really useful knots a boater needs to know with an easy-to-use format.

7

8 BEFORE YOU GET UNDER WAY– ESSENTIAL KNOWLEDGE

Good yacht technique stems from a deep base of essential knowledge. For instance… When do you need to wear a lifejacket or use a harness? How do you tackle a fire? What situations create maximum stress when sailing?

DO YOU NEED A LIFEJACKET?

8

All yachts must be equipped with approved lifejackets for every member of the crew. If you take an RYA sailing course, ranging from Competent Crew to RYA Yachtmaster, it will be normal practice to wear a lifejacket whenever the yacht leaves harbour. If you are enjoying a recreational cruise, including bareboat and flotilla, wearing a lifejacket will be down to personal choice or a request by the skipper. The crew should always wear lifejackets when on deck or in the cockpit at night or in poor visibility. Self-inflating lifejackets are the top choice for use on yachts, with immediate inflation by a CO2 cylinder and the option to top up by blowing into a mouthpiece when you are in the water. Foam lifejackets provide a bulkier alternative. A good approach to take is to wear a lifejacket at all times unless you feel it is safe not to.

Your lifejacket should be fitted with a light, whistle and unused CO2 cylinder. Check that everything works before putting on the lifejacket like a waistcoat. Adjust the waist strap for a precise fit over clothing with the stainless steel buckles locked together. Many lifejackets have a crotch strap to prevent the lifejacket riding up in the water. Always ensure your lifejacket is worn outside all clothing and wet weather gear.

1 Make sure all the straps are the right way round before attaching the buckles.

2 One stainless steel buckle slides through the other buckle at 90 degrees.

3 Pull the buckle back firmly against the other buckle.

4 Adjust waist strap and any crotch straps for a close fit.

WEARING A HARNESS

If you need to wear a lifejacket, you should be ready to clip on with a safety tether. A tether prevents you from falling off the boat, which arguably contributes a lot more to personal safety on the water. The sensible solution is to wear a lifejacket designed to be used with a tether, instead of having to wear a separate harness and lifejacket. The harness line can be stowed in the lifejacket pocket when not in use.

The tether is a heavy duty webbing strap with quick-release clips at both ends. One end is clipped to the waist strap of your lifejacket or harness, while the other end can be clipped to a convenient anchor point on the boat. Look for heavy duty, stainless steel eyes in the cockpit. When moving along the deck, clip the harness line to the jackstay. You can take the harness line round something solid like the mast and clip the end to the waist strap buckle.

A perfectly sited anchor point for a harness just aft of the wheel.

Never clip on to the guardrails or stanchions – they are not strong enough to hold the load if you go over the side and it clearly makes good sense to have your harness line locked onto something further inboard. There are also 3-point tethers available which allow you the option of clipping on with either a long or short line – providing extra security when you are working in exposed areas on deck such as on the bow during a sail change.

You can clip on from the companionway, before moving into the cockpit.

THE IMPORTANCE OF COMMUNICATION

Look ahead and make sure the whole crew is aware of what is going to happen next. They don't want surprises!

Before anything happens on board a yacht, talk it through with your crew to ensure they know exactly what is going to happen and what they need to do. Situations that will require clear briefing and communication include:

■ Preparing the yacht for sea.

■ Leaving a marina berth.

■ Hoisting and unfurling sails.

■ Tacking and gybing.

■ Reefing sails.

■ Dropping and furling sails.

■ Anchoring or picking up a mooring.

■ Approaching a marina berth.

STRESS-FREE SAILING

There is a common belief that the most dangerous situation you can encounter on a yacht is being caught in a violent storm at sea. However, most cruising sailors will never have to face up to this kind of experience for three good reasons:

1 Coastal sailors do not need to go far offshore.

2 Weather forecasts are generally accurate. If the forecast is bad, do not go afloat!

3 Good passage planning should make it relatively easy to head for shelter if the weather turns foul.

The six most stressful situations you are likely to encounter are:

1 Berthing in a strange marina, particularly if it's tightly packed and the wind is blowing hard, making it difficult to moor up without the bows of the yacht being blown the wrong way. If there is an audience, generally in the late afternoon, a less-than-perfect approach can be embarrassing. Taking the time to assess the approach and preparing lines and fenders in advance can help.

Manoeuvres in marinas can be stressful, but things appear well under control here! A large part of the solution is to plan ahead.

2 Fog at sea. Very nasty with minimal visibility and no wind, so your engine drowns out the noise of other vessels. Study the weather forecast carefully to avoid being caught in fog. If you are in fog, radar becomes an invaluable aid to safe navigation. Know your sound signals and head for shallower water if you find yourself caught out.

3 Strong winds. Conditions in Force 6+ tend to be more dangerous close inshore near the coast than offshore in open water where you have plenty of space to ride out the storm on smooth rolling waves. Options may include turning downwind for a more comfortable ride or heaving-to. Force 6+ in shallow water close inshore will tend to create steep, closely spaced waves, which are at best uncomfortable. If the wind gets very strong or the engine fails, the yacht may be driven to leeward with potentially dire consequences. As an example, the famous racing yacht *Morning Cloud III*, owned by British Prime Minister Edward Heath, was driven onto a lee shore while sailing past Selsey Bill in the summer of 1975. The yacht was wrecked and one crew was lost overboard.

4 Tidal race. Sailing through a tidal race at the wrong state of tide can be very unpleasant and potentially dangerous. Typical 'no go' areas with wind against tide flowing in the wrong direction include the infamous Portland Race off Portland Bill and the Alderney Race. Passage planning and tide tables will avoid this problem.

5 Collision course. It can be surprisingly difficult to gauge the closing speed of a ferry or ship, particularly if it is changing course, when crossing a shipping lane or deep water channel. The solution is to keep a safe distance away from shipping and make your intentions clear.

6 Sailing at night. Lights cause the most stress at night, when a keen watch is required to work out the course of other vessels. Close to shore, navigation lights can be tricky to spot amongst the back scatter of lights on shore.

8

FIRE ON BOARD

If a fire on a yacht gets out of control, there is nowhere for the crew to go apart from the sea or liferaft, unless you get rescued by a boat or helicopter. Thankfully, this is an extremely rare occurrence.

The main high risk area is the galley stove.

- Take care with matches.
- Keep flammable material, including your clothing and the drying-up cloth, well away from burner flames.
- Never light burners and leave them unattended.
- Avoid cooking with flammable liquids such as oil to fry chips or brandy for pancakes.
- If there is fire, smother it immediately with the fire blanket.
- Always turn off the gas supply – preferably at the bottle – when not in use.
- Minimise the amount of flammable liquid carried on board and ensure it is stowed securely away from the main cabin.

If fire breaks out, the crew should don lifejackets and assemble on deck with the hand-held VHF and grab-bag for the liferaft. Be prepared to move the liferaft away from the fire. Grab extinguishers from below – they are normally located by the companionway steps and by the main bulkhead leading to the forecabin. Close hatches and vents to minimise the air supply. Try to extinguish the fire at its source, but beware of entering a smoke filled cabin. If the engine is alight, do not let more air boost the flames by removing the companionway steps. Discharge the extinguisher through the fire hole.

Don't hesitate to issue a Mayday – you can always cancel it in the event you get the fire under control.

> ***Other fire risks are likely to be mechanical or electrical. (Smoking on board yachts is not illegal, but do take care!)***

Always turn off the gas supply – preferably at the bottle – when not in use.

COILING ROPES

Any length of rope that is not being used, such as mooring ropes when sailing, should be coiled and stowed neatly away. This ensures that the rope will be ready for immediate use, without snagging and tangling in knots. Most ropes on a yacht are 'braided' with a stretch-resistant core and protective outer layer. 'Stranded' rope provides a cheaper alternative with three or more strands twisted together. Whatever type, the problem is that it will tend to twist into a figure-of-eight when coiled. Use the following technique to create beautifully hung coils!

▤ Start from one end, pull out a full arm's length and twist the rope between thumb and forefinger each time you make a loop. This will help to remove any figure-of-eights. Make each loop the same size and gather them in one hand. If the bunch of loops gets too big to hold, lay it down on the deck and start making a second bunch of loops.

▤ You will need the tail end of the rope to secure the coils. It is better to have too much than too little – an equivalent length to one and a half coils should suffice.

▤ Hold the bunch of coils in one hand and make three or four tight horizontal turns not too far from the top. Make a U-bend with the remaining rope, push it through the hole at the top of the coils and pull through the end of the rope to lock the bunch.

1 Make sure the rope is neatly coiled with no twists.

2 Bunch the coils together towards the top.

3 Take several tight turns around the coils.

4 Push a loop through the top of the coils.

5 Pull back over the top and tighten.

6 You can now hang up the coiled rope.

THROWING ROPES

Typically, you may need to throw a rope when coming alongside a dock. First rule – don't assume people on the dock will be able to catch your rope or know what to do! You will have to assess their potential ability.

The normal problem when throwing a rope is that it falls short and drops in the water, so you have to pull it in and try again. The solution is to use weight. Hold a tight bunch of coils in your throwing hand with a loose bunch of coils in your other hand. Throw the first coil and let the rest of the coils pay out. Aim to the side and beyond the 'catcher' on the dock. You don't want the rope to hit them in the face; you do want it to straddle the dock so they can grab the rope easily.

1 Shake out the rope.

2 Hold your arms wide to make big coils.

3 Make sure there are no twists or snags.

4 Keep coiling until you have enough weight and length to throw.

5 Throw the coils and let the slack rope follow.

FIRING FLARES

Firing flares helps pinpoint the location of a yacht for search and rescue services. It is illegal to fire flares unless summoning assistance in a Mayday emergency, which means there is grave and imminent danger to life or vessel.

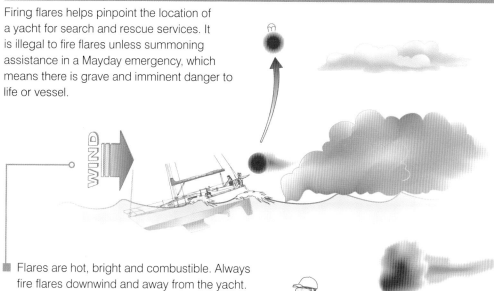

▩ Flares are hot, bright and combustible. Always fire flares downwind and away from the yacht. Hold at arm's length when firing, preferably wearing a thick leather glove. Protect your eyes – never look at a brightly burning flare.

8

▩ Flares should be stored in a watertight container. Each flare must be 'in date' to ensure it will fire correctly. Shelf life is around 3 years.

▩ Orange smoke flares are designed for use in bright daylight. They have a limited range and the smoke may dissipate quickly, unless it is a still day. A floating orange smoke flare next to the boat can have a burn time of 3 minutes, while a hand-held orange smoke flare may burn for less than 1 minute.

▩ Handheld red flares have a burn time of 1–3 minutes and are visible to 3 miles at night or on a dull day. These flares are used to attract attention from nearby vessels or land.

▩ Red parachute flares rocket up to about 300 metres, before the bright red light drifts down on a parachute, providing a potential range up to 25 miles. Fire vertically for maximum height, or at an angle if there is low cloud.

▩ White pinpoint flares are used to indicate collision warning.

SIGNALLING DISTRESS

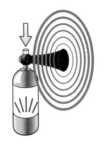

Give a long blast on the foghorn.

Fly a ball and a square flag.

Raise and lower both arms in a steady movement to signal distress. Stand on deck where you can be seen, preferably wearing a high visibility jacket. **Do not use this as part of your daily exercise routine.**

Fly Code Flags N and C which indicate distress.

VHF DSC
Use the DSC (Digital Selective Calling) button on your VHF radio to signal distress, followed by a Mayday voice call.

SOS

Signal SOS with a torch or lamp.
Keep repeating 3 dots 3 dashes 3 dots.

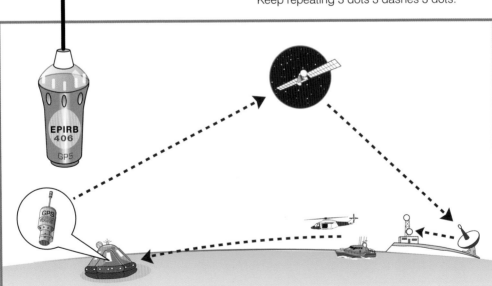

The EPIRB transmits a continuous position signal to the rescue services via satellite and land station. It must float and can transmit for a minimum 48 hours. A personal EPIRB is a miniature version with less sophisticated performance that can be carried in a pocket.

NOT FEELING WELL?

SEASICK

Seasickness is so unfair – some people suffer and others don't. It comes on steadily. As soon as you start to think, "I'm feeling a little bit sick…" things will get worse.

Sailors are more vulnerable to seasickness if they are cold, wet and doing nothing. The typical scenario is to huddle in the cockpit feeling more and more miserable. First, you need to get clothes on before you get cold, which comes on quickly thanks to wind chill on the water. Second, you need to keep busy and be involved in running the yacht. If there is nothing else to do, take a spell on the helm and focus your mind on driving the boat.

- It is easy to feel nauseous if the boat is rolling around while you are in the galley or heads down below, with all hatches and ports closed for sailing and minimal ventilation. Get out on deck and take a spell on the helm!
- If you are feeling sick and there is nothing to do, try putting your head down. Climb into a sleeping bag and enjoy a snooze in a leeward (downhill) berth. This is a great way to warm up and recover.
- If you must be sick, don't be ashamed. Ask for a bucket, use it carefully in the cockpit, then pass it to a friendly crew member who will deposit the contents through the guardrails to leeward. Do not lean over the side to throw up. It is uncomfortable, messy and possibly dangerous.

- By all means try your local chemist for seasickness remedies. Read the instructions carefully and take them in plenty of time. They may help, although side effects can include drowsiness.
- Be careful what you eat. Dry toast or biscuits, plus plenty of water, is a sensible recipe when you are seasick.
- The best news is that most people get over seasickness in time!
- If you think you may be prone to seasickness try and avoid acidic things such as coffee and citrus drinks such as orange juice.

SUNBURN & SUNSTROKE

Beware that sun can be very bright and strong on board a yacht, bouncing off the water and sails. This is a big problem in sailing areas such as Greece and Turkey where the temperature can shoot well past 40C in high summer. The problem is that with a breeze on your body, you may not realise how hot it is until too late, resulting in sunburn, dehydration and possible sunstroke. A bimini which covers the cockpit is ideal for such conditions, but may only provide partial protection for the crew. Go heavy on the sunscreen and cover up sensitive parts of your skin. Drink lots of bottled water – aim for 3 litres or more a day. Wear sunglasses to protect your eyes against strong UV. They will also help postpone the appearance of crow's feet!

Always wear a hat.

8

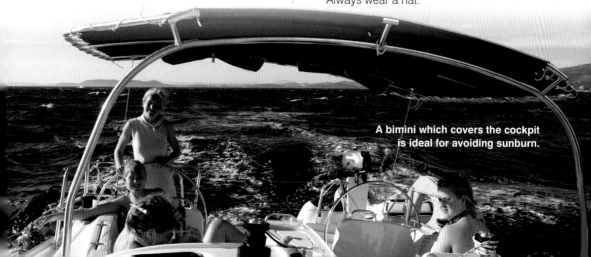

A bimini which covers the cockpit is ideal for avoiding sunburn.

9 PASSAGE PLANNING & NAVIGATION

Yacht navigation is a big subject, which can be complex and is learnt with experience and time. This chapter provides guidelines for safe passage planning and navigation when enjoying modest trips on a yacht.
See page 89 for information on specialist RYA books and courses.

WHY BOTHER WITH TRADITIONAL NAVIGATION?

Traditional paper chart, plotter and a soft pencil are basic requirements for failsafe navigation.

GPS appears to make navigation so easy, particularly with a chartplotter displaying exactly where your yacht is on an electronic chart. With that kind of real-time facility, surely you barely need to bother about navigation at all? If you don't know where you are, just press 'Find yacht'. If the electronic chart shows shallow water or a rock ahead, just turn the wheel and sail out of danger.

There are two problems. Firstly, you need good fundamental knowledge of pilotage and navigation to ensure safe, stress-free sailing. Not bothering to learn is similar to saying, "Why should kids learn maths and spelling when calculators and computers will do it all for them?" Secondly, GPS requires electricity and satellites to function, either of which can switch off or lose contact without warning. Charging through a narrow rocky passage, swept along by a fast tide beneath your keel, is not a good time to suddenly be confronted by a blank GPS with no record of the course on paper, let alone inside your head. GPS is never 100 per cent reliable. On one occasion, I was approaching the Caribbean island of Anegada, which is surrounded by hidden reefs with an unmarked passage leading towards

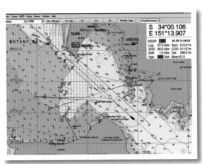

An electronic plotter provides real time navigation on a screen. Make sure it's not virtual reality!

a safe anchorage. The classic method of approaching Anegada is to use a series of transits on the land. It is just as well I was using this method, with a hand-written passage plan in my hand, as one moment the chartplotter was displaying our safe route across the reef and the next moment it was blank. Due to a major software problem, it also stayed that way for the remainder of our two-week cruise!

Modern electronic plotters provide very clear graphics but it is essential not to be lulled into a false sense of security. Ensure you understand the basic principles of navigation and always back up your GPS or plotter position with a secondary means of position fixing such as transits, visual checks of buoyage and landmarks or a check of the depth.

A solution is always to back-up electronic navigation by plotting your route on a paper chart. Use a plastic plotter to measure bearings and brass dividers to measure distance to each point on the route. Use a pilot book to research the coastal area and decide how to make landfalls. If you are sailing in a tidal area, use tide tables to work out which way and how fast the tide will be flowing, as well as how much water will be under your keel. Your route should be plotted on the chart with a soft pencil. It should also be recorded in a notebook as a 'Passage Plan' providing details of bearings, distances and changes in direction, as well as tidal effects, danger areas, buoyage, conspicuous objects on land, transits and how to make the final approach to a harbour.

This could provide an hour's enjoyable work at the chart table. Then you are ready to input your route as GPS waypoints, with the ability to check between GPS, paper chart and passage plan while you are sailing. If they don't agree, you will know something is wrong!

PLANNING A ROUTE

A cautious navigator is a successful navigator. A passage through a beautiful island archipelago may look straightforward on a sunny day, but appearances can be deceptive and conditions may change in a very short time. Our cautious navigator will need a lot of knowledge to ensure a safe passage:

- Optimum course to steer between waypoints with distances and ETA following each change of direction.
- How close to sail to the islands without risk of going aground.
- Timing and effects of tide flowing with or against the boat.
- Tidal races and tidal gates which must be avoided.
- How wind and sea conditions are likely to develop during the passage, thanks to the weather forecast.
- Possible local meteorological effects such as accelerated wind off high hills.

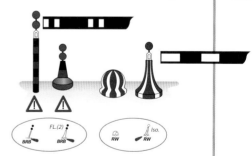

Isolated Danger Mark   **Safe Water Mark**

- Channel markers and lights to watch out for.
- Nearby anchorages or harbours which will provide shelter in different wind directions if conditions deteriorate or the crew do not wish to sail any further.

BE PREPARED

A good navigator should work out the route long before the yacht leaves dock, making full use of the correct charts, tide tables and nautical almanac or pilot book. Potential hazards, which can be analysed with the pilot book and chart, may include:

- Dangerous rocks and shallows.
- Shipping lanes and channels.
- Chain ferries which create an underwater obstruction.

- How different states of the tide will affect your passage, either through tidal flow or underwater dangers.

Preparation will include listening to weather forecasts indicating wind speed, direction and sea state for the area, broadcast on the radio or by the regional Coastguard on VHF, paying particular attention to storm warnings on Channel 16. You can also check forecasts on the web, for instance with an iPhone, or forecasts posted by the harbourmaster.

Be particularly careful when navigating in or near shipping lanes. Be sure that your intentions are made clear to any ships you will be passing close to.

GPS WAYPOINTS FOR YOUR ROUTE

■ The Global Positioning System uses a constellation of satellites circling the earth. At least three satellites are required to provide a GPS receiver with a fix, which can be accurate to within a few metres.

■ Waypoints are points along a route. The latitude and longitude of each waypoint can be stored in the GPS receiver, which will calculate distance, bearing and ETA for each waypoint.

■ It is easy to enter an incorrect number with the slip of a finger! Make sure the latitude and longitude of each waypoint is correctly entered on the GPS, then check distances and bearings against the route you have plotted on a paper chart. This is also an important precaution if you have entered waypoints taken from a publication such as a pilot book or from the web. They may be incorrect!

■ Plot your waypoints close to targets such as buoys or headlands, rather than directly on top of them. This avoids the possibility of sailing directly into something solid with all your faith resting on the GPS. Remember that dozens of other navigators could be using the same waypoints, so look out for them as you converge in a popular boating area.

■ Make sure that your route between waypoints sticks to water. This is not as silly as it sounds. A GPS will follow the route you have requested, with no idea of the vital difference between rock and sea! Believe it or not, yachts have attempted to sail through headlands with autopilot linked to GPS and the crew taking it easy down below. Unsurprisingly, they have come to grief because of this basic delusion.

9

REAL LIFE NAVIGATION?

A multifunction plotter provides a real-time view of your passage on an electronic chart, which is directly linked to GPS. Standard features include storage for more than a thousand waypoints and a hundred pre-formatted routes, using charts from around the globe. It is easy to look at the screen and be mesmerised as the plotter shows your boat steadily moving along the route. But don't forget to use your eyes in real-life as well! Go on deck, look for buoys or landmarks, take bearings, check your depth, record your position on the chart or in the log.

APPROACHING LAND

Accurate navigation is crucial as you approach land. As you move from open water to the confines of narrower and shallower channels and harbours you change from 'navigation' to 'pilotage'. This is essentially 'eyeball navigation' and relies heavily on good preparation of a pilotage plan with effective use of visual aids that will be easy to identify along the way.

BUOYS MARK THE CHANNEL

Lateral buoys or markers are red or green. Red should be left to port and green to starboard when entering a port or travelling upstream in an IALA A region. Leave red to starboard and green to port when leaving the channel.

- A fairway buoy or marker has red and white vertical stripes, indicating safe water at the end of a channel.
- An isolated danger buoy or marker has red and black bands with two black balls.
- Special buoys or markers are yellow with a cross, indicating an area such as speed limit or dumping areas.

Red buoy on the right on the way out of a harbour.

Red pillar with red flashing light marks the port side of a harbour entrance.

Green pillar with green flashing light marks the starboard side of a harbour entrance.

Yellow or orange buoys mark a special area.

White pillar with flashing light marking an offshore rock in Croatia.

KEEP CLEAR OF THIS AREA

Cardinal buoys or markers identify nearby danger areas. Unlike lateral marks, they are used in exactly the same way in both IALA A and IALA B areas. The location of the danger is indicated by yellow and black colours with arrows indicating direction on top of the mark. The cardinal pillar shown in this photo indicates a danger area immediately to the south.

Pass to the north, danger to the south: Arrows point up + yellow/black. Continuous quick white flash by night.

Pass to the south, danger to the north: Arrows point down + black/yellow. 6+1 long white flashes.

Pass to the west, danger to the east: Arrows point inwards + yellow/black/yellow. 9 white flashes.

Pass to the east, danger to the west: Arrows point outwards + black/yellow/black. 3 white flashes.

9

IALA

The International Association of Lighthouse Authorities divides the world into two areas.

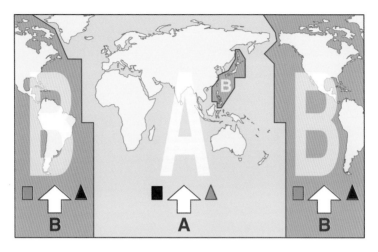

IALA **A**

IALA **B**

Europe, Africa, Australia, India and most of Asia use System A: Leave red lateral marks to port and green lateral marks to starboard when entering harbour. Leave red to starboard and green to port when leaving.

America and South-East Asia use System B: Leave green lateral marks to port and red lateral marks to starboard when entering harbour. Leave green to starboard and red to port when leaving.

Red marks flash red. Green marks flash green.

STARBOARD SIDE IN, STARBOARD SIDE OUT

Keep to the starboard side of the channel and allow larger vessels to use deep water in the centre. Your passage planning must include a depth check for your estimated time of arrival, particularly if there is a large rise and fall of tide. Beware of cutting corners and missing out markers if the channel weaves from side to side. Always look ahead and spot the next port and starboard markers. If you hit the mud on a falling tide, you risk waiting for as long as 12 hours to lift back off!

Choose the right time to leave a narrow channel. Steer to starboard if there is an approaching vessel.

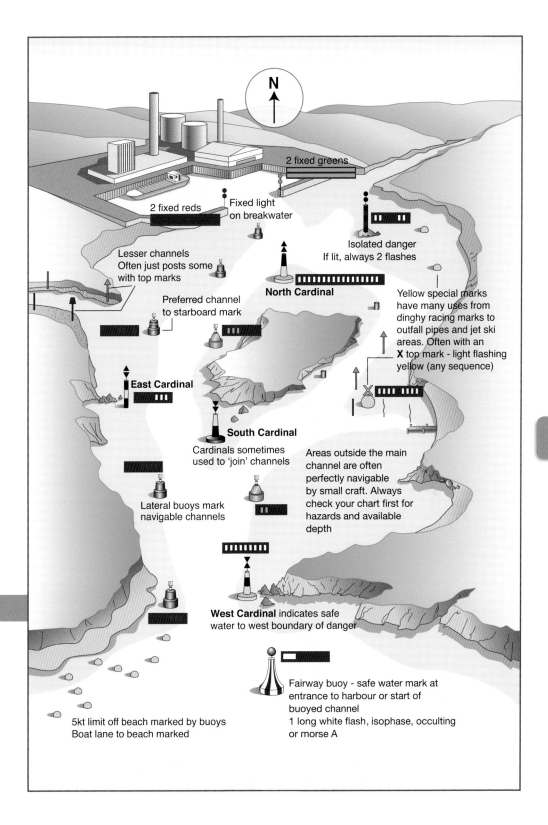

N

2 fixed greens

2 fixed reds

Fixed light
on breakwater

Isolated danger
If lit, always 2 flashes

Lesser channels
Often just posts some
with top marks

Preferred channel
to starboard mark

North Cardinal

Yellow special marks
have many uses from
dinghy racing marks to
outfall pipes and jet ski
areas. Often with an
X top mark - light flashing
yellow (any sequence)

East Cardinal

South Cardinal

Cardinals sometimes
used to 'join' channels

Areas outside the main
channel are often
perfectly navigable
by small craft. Always
check your chart first for
hazards and available
depth

Lateral buoys mark
navigable channels

West Cardinal indicates safe
water to west boundary of danger

Fairway buoy - safe water mark at
entrance to harbour or start of
buoyed channel
1 long white flash, isophase, occulting
or morse A

5kt limit off beach marked by buoys
Boat lane to beach marked

9

ANNOUNCE YOUR ARRIVAL

As soon as you are within radio range, use the VHF channel listed in the pilot book to make contact with the harbourmaster or marina berthing manager. Alternatively, it may be possible to 'book in' with a mobile phone. Request directions on how to proceed to a berth. You will receive instructions on where to go and whether to have warps and fenders ready on the port or starboard side.

IDENTIFY LANDMARKS

Major landmarks are marked on the chart and provide an important reference when closing on the shore. Use transits and bearings as part of your passage plan.

The Spinnaker Tower provides a fine landmark near the entrance to Portsmouth Harbour. Careful planning is required to enter this extremely busy naval and commercial harbour with strongly enforced exclusion zones.

9

Having contacted the marina, the crew know they need to prepare fenders and warps on the port side.

BEWARE OF LARGE VESSELS

On-water traffic will increase when approaching a busy harbour. Take bearings to other vessels using a hand-bearing compass. If bearings do not change significantly a risk of collision exists. Be aware that ships will follow the main channel and may change course.

HOW TO BECOME A NAVIGATOR

TAKE A COURSE

To learn the fundamentals of navigation, take an RYA course:

RYA Day Skipper Theory

A shore-based course with topics including:
- Basics of seamanship.
- Essentials of coastal navigation and pilotage.
- Chartwork.
- Electronic charts.
- Position fixing.
- Plotting a course to steer.
- Weather forecasting and meteorology.
- Tides.
- Collision regulations.
- Construction, parts and equipment of a cruising boat.
- Emergency and safety procedures including distress calls, use of flares, safety harnesses, lifejackets and liferafts.

The course is taught over 40 hours and includes two exams. It can range from an intensive week to winter evening classes spread over two terms.

RYA Day Coastal Skipper/RYA Yachtmaster Offshore Theory

An advanced shore-based course with topics including:
- Position fixing.
- Course shaping and plotting.
- Tidal knowledge.
- Use of almanacs and Admiralty publications.
- Electronic position-finding equipment.
- Taking and interpreting forecasts.
- Plotting weather systems.
- Weather predictions using a barometer and by observation.
- Collision regulations.
- Customs and immigration regulations for cruising abroad.

The course is taught over 40 hours and includes three exams. It can range from an intensive week to winter evening classes spread over two terms.

9

READ A BOOK

Recommended books on navigation and pilotage:

RYA Navigation Handbook (G6) by Melanie Bartlett
Equal weighting on electronic and traditional navigation for yachts.

RYA Navigation Exercises (G7) by Chris Slade
In line with RYA courses including vital aspects of seamanship. Chris Slade is co-author of Day Skipper and RYA Yachtmaster test papers.

RYA Day Skipper Shorebased Course Notes (DSN)
Essential reading for anyone taking the beginners' course in navigation, safety and seamanship. Small format is ideal for keeping ready-to-hand on a yacht.

Day Skipper Practical Course Notes (DSPCN)
Navigation, safety and seamanship techniques for taking charge of a yacht for a short passage. Small format is ideal for keeping ready-to-hand on a yacht.

RYA International Regulations for Preventing Collisions at Sea (G2) by Melanie Bartlett
Invaluable yachtsman's guide to all the rules.

WHO SHOULD GIVE WAY?

POWER & SAIL

- A power-driven vessel must give way to a craft under sail, which must give way to a vessel fishing, which must give way to a vessel constrained by draught, which must give way to a vessel restricted in ability to manoeuvre.

- This means that when sailing on board a yacht, a power-driven vessel should give way to you. You must give way to fishing boats that are trawling, vessels that cannot change course due to shallow water and vessels that cannot change course while they are engaged in work such as laying channel markers or dredging.

- If a yacht is motoring, it is considered to be a power-driven vessel. If a yacht under sail overtakes a power-driven vessel, it must keep clear.

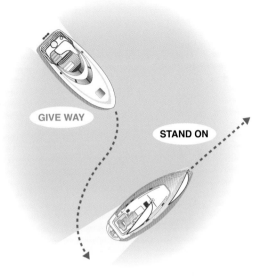

SAIL

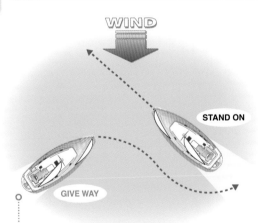

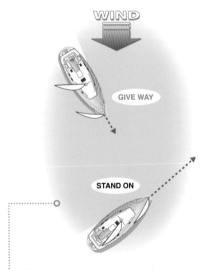

- When two sailing vessels meet on different tacks, the vessel on port tack must give way to the vessel on starboard tack. The port tack boat should take avoiding action by tacking, slowing down or bearing away.

- When two boats meet on the same tack, the windward side boat must keep clear. This means that a yacht sailing on a reach or run must give way to a same tack yacht that is beating upwind.

POWER

- Overtaking boat keeps clear.

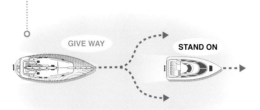

- When two vessels are approaching one another head-on, both should alter course to starboard, passing one another 'port to port'.

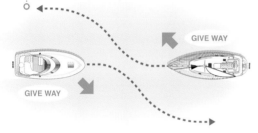

- When two boats are converging, the starboard side boat has right of way. The easiest way to remember this rule is to think of port (red) and starboard (green) navigation lights. If you see the green light side of the other boat's bows, you are the stand-on vessel. They will see the red light side of your bows and must give way.

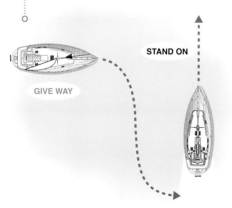

NEVER RISK A COLLISION

- Always keep a proper lookout. Beware of blind spots behind the sails. Keep your speed under control, particularly under engine in a crowded harbour.
- Use a hand-bearing compass to check converging course with another vessel. Take a succession of bearings from the same point on your yacht – for instance, lining up the compass with a fixed point on the vessel of interest. If the bearings do not change, you are on collision course and should take avoiding action.

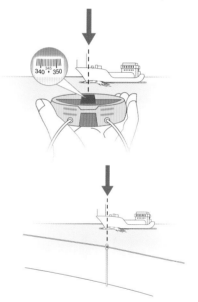

- Make your intentions clear. If you are changing course to avoid collision, make an obvious turn to port or starboard. Do not just change course by a few degrees.
- A ship will use sound signals to indicate a change in course which may affect other craft.

   1 short blast = turning to starboard
   2 blasts = turning to port
   3 blasts = engines astern

- It can be difficult to judge the speed of an approaching ship. If there is any doubt of crossing ahead, always cross astern and keep well clear of the wash.

LIGHTS AT NIGHT

Most vessels will show red (port/left), green (starboard/right) and white (stern) lights at night.

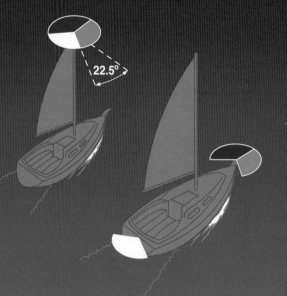

22.5°

When motoring, turn on the white steaming light which is mounted on the mast. Use a steaming light in conjunction with a bicolour pulpit light, but not with a masthead tricolour light.

9 A yacht (less than 20 metres length) under sail must show a tricolour red/green/white light at the masthead or bicolour red/green light mounted on the pulpit and single white light at the stern.

When sailing at night, shore lights can be extremely confusing with masses of street lights obscuring the flashing channel markers and harbour entrance lights. It is important to identify the correct navigational lights and keep them in sight with hand-held bearings. Stand off until you can make a positive identification. Strong wind and driving rain would make this approach a lot more difficult!

FIXED NAVIGATION LIGHTS

Lighthouses are identified by different light patterns with specific time intervals:
Single flashes = less light than dark
Group flashes
Fixed light
Occulting = more light than dark
Isophase = equal light and dark

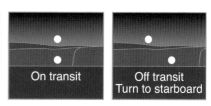

Off transit
Turn to port

On transit

Off transit
Turn to starboard

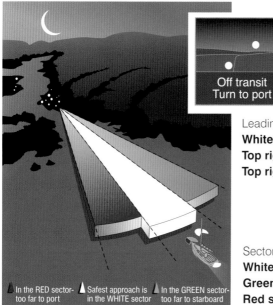

In the RED sector- too far to port

Safest approach is in the WHITE sector

In the GREEN sector- too far to starboard

Leading lights guide craft in and out of a harbour:
White above white = you are on course
Top right to the right = you are too far to starboard
Top right to the left = you are too far to port

Sector lights have three colours:
White sector = you are on course
Green sector = you are too far to starboard
Red sector = you are too far to port

9

Charts provide information on light characteristics. For instance:
Iso. WR. 4s 20m 10 / 7M = Isophase White Red every 4 seconds 20 metres above Mean High Water Springs White visible 10 miles / Red visible 7 miles in good conditions.

NAME	CHART SYMBOL	DESCRIPTION	VISUALLY
Fixed	F	Fixed light - always on	
Flashing	Fl	Flashing, off more than on	
Group flashing	Fl (2)	Flashing in groups	
Long flashing	LFl	Flashing, off more than on but on lasting 2 or more seconds	
Quick	Q	50 - 79 flashes per min	
Very quick	VQ	80 - 90 flashes per min	
Isophase	Iso	Equally on and off	
Occulting	Oc	More on than off	
Alternating	Al.WR	Colour changes	

10 OPERATING THE ENGINE & BASIC MAINTENANCE

A diesel engine provides auxiliary power for a cruising yacht. It not only turns the propeller, but also charges the batteries for fundamental requirements including lights, pressurised water, cold food storage, anchor windlass, VHF radio and electronic navigation.

ENGINE CONTROLS

- The control panel is usually located in the cockpit. It should be within easy reach of the helm and is often recessed into the side of the cockpit.
- Typical features include ignition, engine revs dial, battery charge and oil pressure gauges, warning lights and audible alarms for engine overheating or low oil pressure, fuel level gauge, T-shaped lever pulled out to stop the engine.
- Most modern diesel engines can be started by turning an ignition key, with a short pause to allow for glow plug warming. Older marine diesels may have an ignition key and starter button.

The control panel is located in the cockpit.

STARTING THE ENGINE

Make sure the engine battery – normally by the companionway – is turned on. Do not turn it off when the engine is running. The combined throttle and gearshift lever is ideally mounted on the binnacle, just by the helm's right hand. Operation is very simple.

- Make sure the lever is in the vertical position with the red button at the base of the lever protruding.
- Push in the red button to disengage forward and reverse gears so the propeller will not turn.

10

STOPPING THE ENGINE

Turning the ignition key to the 'off' position will normally not stop a marine diesel engine. Pull the T-shaped stop lever – normally adjacent to the engine control panel or mounted on the binnacle – fully out until the engine stops. Then turn off the ignition key and push in the stop lever.

Do not confuse the stop lever with a fuel cut-off lever, which may also be mounted on the binnacle for use in an emergency such as an engine fire.

Pull the T-shaped stop lever fully out.

Make sure other members of the crew are familiar with engine controls. When the skipper is busy, it can be useful to ask someone to turn the engine on or off, with the ability to use forward or reverse gears.

- Push the throttle lever forward to about 2 o'clock to provide sufficient revs when starting the engine.
- Turn the ignition key to the right and hold it until the engine has started. Alternatively, turn the key and hold in the ignition button. In cold conditions it may be necessary to wait up to 30 seconds for the glow plugs to warm up.
- As soon as the engine is running smoothly, pull the lever back to the vertical position so that the central red button pops out. If you push the lever forward, the propeller will drive the boat ahead. If you pull the lever back, the propeller will drive the boat astern. You should run your engine at about two-thirds of maximum revs for 'cruising speed'.
- Check the safety lights on the control panel for oil pressure, temperature and battery charging. Lean over the stern to check that a steady stream of cooling water is being pumped out of the exhaust. No cooling water indicates the engine will overheat and shut down! An audible alarm may also indicate overheating or lack of oil pressure.

10

Turn ignition key and push start button.

Check cooling water is being pumped through the engine.

Always allow extra fuel for a cruise – do not risk running out of diesel which will cause all kinds of problems

CHECKING FUEL

- Check the fuel gauge when the engine is running and keep a record of engine hours, which provides a vital double-check in case the fuel gauge is inaccurate. You can work out how many litres the engine will use each hour by referring to the manual.

- Do not risk running out diesel fuel. Air will get into the fuel supply and you will be unable to restart without first bleeding the fuel system. Refer to the manual for instructions. Be warned that bleeding air out of the engine and restarting could be extremely difficult in a rough sea.

- Always allow extra fuel for a cruise. Calculate how much is required and then add 30 per cent. Keep a full can of diesel fuel in a cockpit locker as an emergency reserve.

FILLING UP

The diesel filler is clearly marked on the deck. Come alongside the fuel pontoon on the correct side. Do not spill fuel over the side or on the deck. Take particular care that no water gets into the fuel tank.

Most marinas have a fuel berth that is easy to come alongside near the entrance.

MOTORING

- When shifting between forward and reverse gears, or vice-versa, pause briefly in neutral. Do not pull the lever from gear-to-gear in one movement.
- The higher the revs, the more diesel you will burn. It will also be noisier with higher levels of vibration, both in the cockpit and below deck. Above a certain speed, this may be counter-productive. Increasing revs to the maximum in forward gear will

Don't pull the lever from gear-to-gear in one movement.

suck the stern into the water without the yacht travelling any faster. Little more than 2,000 revs should provide an economical cruising speed.

- The propeller shaft may spin when the yacht is under sail with the engine turned off. This is due to the propeller being dragged through the water. The whirring noise can get quite annoying. An easy solution is to pull the gearshift back so the shaft is locked in reverse gear.

The inverted triangle indicates that this yacht is motorsailing.

10

ENGINE CHECKS

Refer to the manual for specific engine checks. Regular checks may include:

- Engine oil – check dipstick level while the engine is warm but after it has had some time to cool a little.
- Freshwater cooling – top up with anti-freeze mixture as required.
- Raw water filter – close cooling water seacock and remove debris that has been sucked in by the engine.
- Fuel filter – clean out water or dirt, if accessible.
- Drive belts – check tension and condition.
- Hoses – check exhaust and cooling water hoses for damage.
- Gearbox oil – check dipstick level.

Remove the companionway ladder for regular checks on the engine. You may also need to remove an access panel in the aft cabin.

10

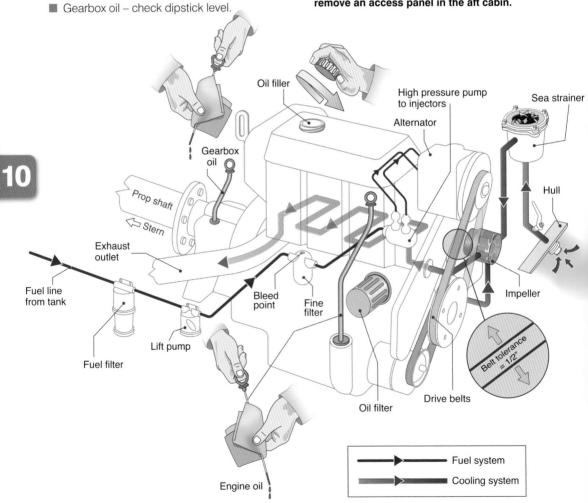

Oil filler

High pressure pump to injectors

Sea strainer

Alternator

Gearbox oil

Hull

Prop shaft

Stern

Exhaust outlet

Impeller

Fuel line from tank

Bleed point

Fine filter

Belt tolerance = 1/2"

Lift pump

Fuel filter

Drive belts

Oil filter

Engine oil

Fuel system

Cooling system

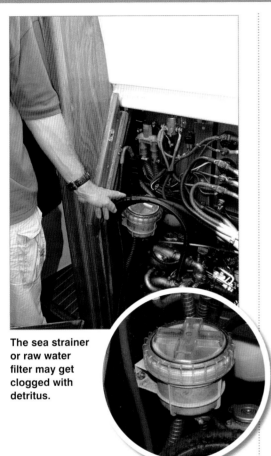

The sea strainer or raw water filter may get clogged with detritus.

Check that belts are not heavily worn or stretched.

A good tool kit and spares are essential.

TAKE A COURSE

RYA Diesel Engine Course

One-day beginners' course designed to prevent and solve diesel engine failure. Course topics include:

- Principles of diesel engine operation.
- Systems and parts of the engine.
- Fault finding.
- Rectification of common problems.
- Bleeding the fuel system.
- Changing the impeller.
- Routine maintenance.
- Winter lay-up procedures.

READ A BOOK

RYA Diesel Engine Handbook (G25) by Andrew Simpson

How the engine works, maintenance, troubleshooting, DIY mechanics. Essential reading for the RYA Diesel Engine Course.

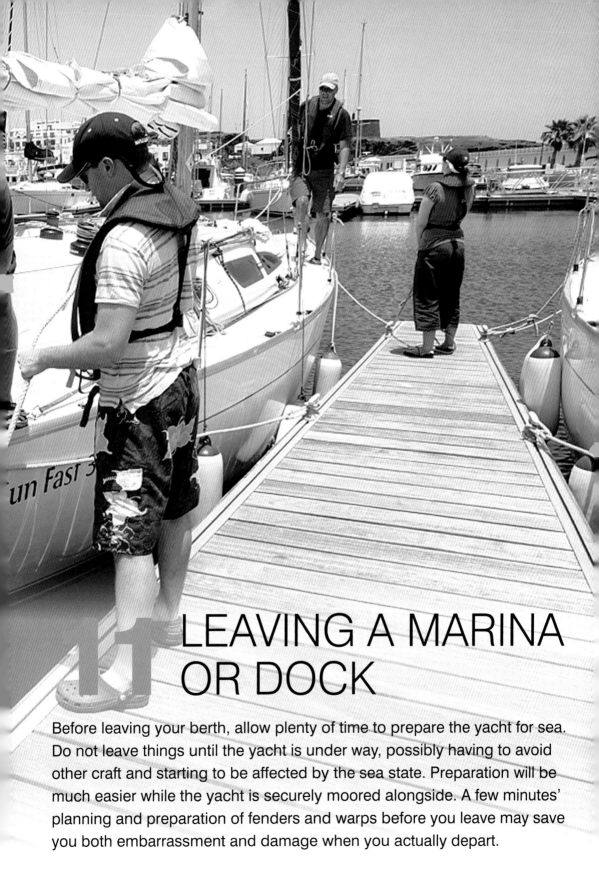

11 LEAVING A MARINA OR DOCK

Before leaving your berth, allow plenty of time to prepare the yacht for sea. Do not leave things until the yacht is under way, possibly having to avoid other craft and starting to be affected by the sea state. Preparation will be much easier while the yacht is securely moored alongside. A few minutes' planning and preparation of fenders and warps before you leave may save you both embarrassment and damage when you actually depart.

PREPARING TO LEAVE

MAINSAIL

The mainsail is held securely by ties while the cover is folded back along the boom.

11

If the mainsail has a conventional cover, remove it starting from the mast. There is normally a zip on the front, a tie at the top and elastics all the way along the bottom of the cover. Fold the cover back along the boom. Lift it off the boom and fold into a neat bundle that stows inside a cockpit locker.

Many cruising yachts are fitted with lazy jacks and a stack-pack. Lazy jacks are a spider's web of lines on either side of the mainsail. When the mainsail is being hoisted or lowered, the lazy jacks help to centralise it above the boom. A stack-pack is the bag that catches the mainsail as it is lowered between the lazy jacks, with deep canvas flaps either side of the boom and a long zip to close the flaps over the lowered sail. You will need to undo this zip as a prelude to hoisting the sail.

Stack-pack and lazy jacks make it as easy as possible to hoist or lower the mainsail.

MAIN HALYARD

It is good practice to attach the halyard, so the mainsail is ready for immediate hoisting when you leave the dock. Firstly, it is much easier to attach the halyard when the yacht is stable. Secondly, it may be necessary to hoist the mainsail without delay if the engine fails.

When not in use, the main halyard is normally attached to the end of the boom. This ensures it will not drive everyone crazy by clanking against the aluminium mast on a windy night! Ease off the main halyard, which will be led through a clutch on the coachroof. Undo the shackle attaching the halyard to the end of the boom and walk it forward to the mast. You will need some slack on the halyard, but beware of letting a loose halyard blow round the front of the spreaders – it can be surprisingly difficult to flick back. Don't let the halyard go or it may blow away from the boat. If this happens, try using the boat hook to pull it back. When attaching the shackle to the headboard of the mainsail, push in the pin and turn through 180 degrees to ensure it is securely locked.

How do you tension the halyard to stop it flailing around and pulling part of the mainsail up the mast? One solution is to pull a one metre length of halyard down around any convenient cleat on the mast, then tension and lock off the halyard. Another is to lead the halyard under a sail tie closest to the mast, then up to the headboard. Either method will pull the head down and keep the mainsail ready for immediate hoisting.

When not in use, the main halyard is normally attached to the end of the boom.

Push in the pin and turn through 180°.

Lead the halyard under a sail tie.

11

SAIL TIES

A conventional mainsail is held by sail-ties round the boom, which can be removed in seconds. On a yacht with lazy jacks and a stack-pack, sail ties are unnecessary. The mainsail simply lies inside the stack-pack.

◄ **The mainsail is held by sail-ties round the boom.**

MAINSHEET

Unhitch the coiled mainsheet from the boom and lay the coils in the cockpit, ensuring the sheet will be able to run free when the sail is hoisted.

MAINSAIL REEFING PENNANTS

If you are hoisting full mainsail, the reefing lines or 'pennants' must be able to run free when the sail is hoisted. Best practice is to open the clutches for each pennant. Be prepared to pull the pennants through by hand, as there is a lot of friction. Only keep these clutches closed if you wish to maintain a reef in the sail.

PREPARE CONTROL LINES

All ropes used to control the rig should be ready for use. Lift coils off the coachroof winches and drop them down either side of the companionway, ensuring each rope can run free. This may appear messy, but it is preferable to have loose ropes well away from the cockpit floor where they are likely to get caught under feet. Once the sails are hoisted you may wish to tidy up by putting the tails of your halyards and other control lines in rope bags or 'rope tidies' in the cockpit.

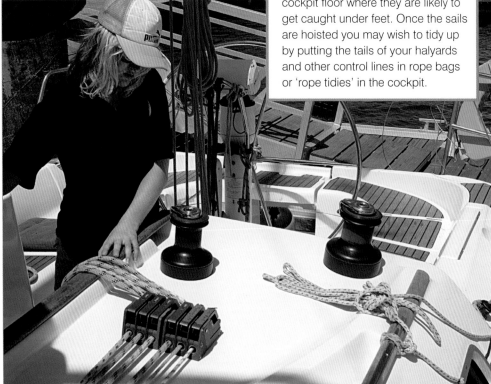

Halyards, reefing lines and other control lines must be able to run free, without obstructing the crew.

MOORING ROPES

The yacht shown in the photos has been moored alongside the pontoon with warps and springs attached to cleats on the pontoons by bowlines. This is neat and secure for a long stay in the marina, but the ropes will need to be changed for the easiest possible departure.

■ Change the bow and stern warps (ropes used to hold the boat alongside) to slip ropes. This means that both ends of the warp will be attached to a bow or stern cleat, with a single loop round the nearest cleat on the dock. The obvious method is to attach one end of each warp to a cleat on the yacht, lead it through the nearest fairlead and down round the cleat on the

The stern warp is looped round the dock cleat for easy departure as shown on page 102.

pontoon, then back to the same cleat on the yacht. The problem is that when the helm says "Let go!", there may be 10 metres or more of rope which has to run round the cleat on the pontoon. Letting go of the long end is asking for trouble – the longer the rope, the more likely it is to snag and jam round the base of the cleat as the yacht moves away from the dock. Even if it does not jam, there will be a surprising amount of friction. Always make sure the short end of the rope (2–3 metres maximum) can be let go first and will pull round the cleat in seconds. Ensure you remove the bowline from the end of the mooring line before slipping or you may find it snags on the dock.

■ Remove the bow and stern springs (ropes used to prevent the yacht moving fore and aft), shortly before you are ready to leave the dock.

Removing the stern spring and looping the stern warp around the dock cleat for easy departure.

11

The yacht is moored to the pontoon with bow and stern lines plus fore and aft springs.

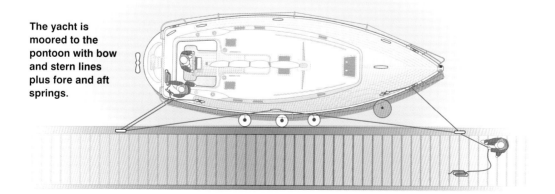

DOWN BELOW

DO NOT OPEN THIS
HATCH AT SEA

**All hatches and vents should be closed.
Make sure levers or clips are in the fully
dogged position.**

■ All hatches and ports
must be closed when
going to sea. Make sure
that both levers are fully
dogged (but not locked) – turned
though 90 degrees – to ensure water
cannot get in. Never lock hatches when at
sea, in case you need to open them from
above in the event of an emergency.

■ Check that everything is neatly stowed
and all cabins are secure. Put all galley
equipment away and do not leave washing-
up in the sink! Make sure the lockers and
drawers are locked closed and cannot fly
open. Stow heavy items carefully – on one
scary occasion, I saw a heavy tool box hurl
itself across the saloon when the yacht had
an unexpected roll. Do not leave anything
loose on the saloon table, because for sure
it will fall onto the floor. Clear all clutter from
the chart table. Beware of leaving clothing
on the saloon seats which will fall onto the
floor. If you stand on it when the boat is
heeling, you will slide.

FOOD AND DRINK

■ Will you need food or drink while sailing? It
is always best to prepare food in advance.
Go for simplicity – such as filled rolls and
snack-bars – so it's easy to grab food and
feed the crew when the yacht is under way.

ON DECK

Disconnect the shore power cable, coil it carefully and stow in the cockpit locker.

■ You must disconnect shore power before leaving the berth. Trailing an electric cable will be extremely embarrassing, at best! Pull out the plug on the dock first, then coil the cable and stow it neatly in a cockpit locker.

■ Close the rear guardrails which are there to stop people falling off the stern. Make sure the helmsman's seat is secured in position.

11

SAFETY FIRST

Lifejackets should always be worn in bad weather or poor visibility. In normal conditions they provide extra security, particularly when combined with a harness and safety tether. Lock the front buckle and tension the waist strap for a trim fit. On this lifejacket the safety tether is neatly folded into a pocket with the clip ready for immediate use.

LEAVING THE BERTH

MOORING ROPES

11

The crew will slip the stern line and bow line when the helm motors slowly ahead. If you let go with the shortest ends, both ropes should slide easily round the cleats on the pontoon. Make sure you pull any loose ends on board as quickly as possible. Never let a rope trail in the water anywhere near the propeller!

Coil all ropes on deck and stow them in cockpit lockers for immediate use. When making a coil, start from one end of the rope. Pull out an arm's length and twist with forefinger and thumb as you catch each coil with the other hand, helping to prevent the coils from forming figure-of-eights. When you have coiled most of the rope, use the remainder to take three or four tight turns round the coils. Finish off by pulling a loop through the top of the coils and locking off with the bitter end.

Coil all ropes on deck and stow them in cockpit lockers for immediate use.

STEERING

Marinas are like car parks. There may be rows of tightly packed yachts with limited room to manoeuvre. Frequently, the helm will need to make a 90 degree turn to port or starboard as soon as the yacht is clear of its berth, in order to avoid the next line of yachts.

Engine ahead

1/3

2/3

PIVOT POINTS
Always remember that the stern moves outwards as the yacht turns around its keel. More power and greater speed will improve steerage and tighten the turn. This is likely to be particularly important in stronger winds, since the bow will tend to 'blow off' with the wind. Getting it right depends on the correct compromise between power and control. If you motor ahead slowly, the yacht will react slowly and turn in a wide arc. If you

motor ahead fast, the yacht will react faster and turn in a tighter arc, but will be heading straight at the next line of yachts for a few worrying seconds. Experience is required to get relaxed about handling a yacht in a tightly packed marina – the more you do it, the easier it becomes.

2/3

1/3

Plan ahead and try to use the wind to your advantage when manoeuvring the boat.

Keep to the right when leaving or entering the marina.

Engine reverse

Use only as much throttle as you need to maintain effective steerage, and watch for other boats on the move. Pay particular attention to ferries and other commercial craft. They can arrive and leave quickly and do not have either the visibility or manoeuvrability of small recreational craft.

ON SUBMARINA - GLASS BOTTOM

Pay particular attention to ferries and other commercial craft.

11

FENDERS

It is a wise precaution to leave fenders in place until you are clear of the marina pontoons. Lift fenders onto the side deck before untying from the guardrails. Fenders are best stowed in cockpit lockers, but take up a lot of space. If there's a problem, tie them onto the pushpit railings, where they are out of the way when sailing. Use a clove hitch to attach each fender securely.

1 Learn to tie a clove hitch using one hand – it's the most useful knot for securing fenders.

Lift fenders onto the side deck before untying from the guardrails.

The clove hitch is quick and easy to tie or untie, as well as secure. Make sure you learn to tie this knot properly.

2 Lay the fender on the side deck and take one complete turn round the guardrail wire.

3 Catch the rope on the other side and pull it back through the loop to lock the clove hitch.

4 The clove hitch is totally secure, but is easy to untie or adjust length to get the fender at the right height.

COCKPIT LOCKERS

A spring-loaded button ensures that the cockpit locker lid stays firmly shut. Press and lift to open, but beware that cockpit locker lids are heavy, have sharp edges and may blow back with a gust of wind when the yacht is on the move. If you are stowing away mooring ropes and fenders, make sure the lid is securely held open – there is often a security line which clips onto the guardrail – before risking your neck or fingers. If necessary, get someone to physically hold the lid open for you.

11

◀ **A spring-loaded button ensures that the cockpit locker lid stays firmly shut. Make sure the lid is securely held open.**

12 MANOEUVRES IN MARINAS

Successful boat handling in a crowded, tightly packed marina requires forethought and care. Plenty of practice will also help you to predict exactly what the yacht can and will do.

DO'S & DON'TS

- **DO** call up the marina before you arrive and ask if it is possible to book a berth. As you approach the marina, call up again. The berthing master should tell you where to go and whether to put warps and fenders on the port or starboard side. With luck, he will be waiting to take your lines.

- **DO** moor alongside the visitors' pontoon, if you don't know where to go in the marina. Walk to the harbourmaster's office, complete the paperwork and use the opportunity to reconnoitre your berth.

- **DO** tell your crew exactly what is going to happen, before approaching your berth. Nominate responsibility for managing bow and stern lines and securing the yacht.

- **DO** assess where the wind is blowing and where the tide is flowing. You don't want to be driven onto a line of moored yachts by losing sufficient space to manoeuvre due to strong wind or tide.

- **DO** be considerate to your marina neighbours.

- **DO NOT** arrive in a strange marina unannounced or late in the day. It may be full-up with yachts, whose crews will enjoy watching you attempting to manoeuvre into a particularly tight berth. Most marinas are emptiest and quietest in the early afternoon.

- **DO NOT** try sailing inside a marina. It could have embarrassing results. However, be prepared to unfurl part of the headsail or hoist the mainsail in case the engine suddenly fails.

- **DO NOT** motor around at full speed inside a marina. You need just enough speed to keep way on with proper control of your boat.

- **DO NOT** raft up alongside other boats before checking with their owners.

Moor alongside the visitors' pontoon if you have not been allocated a berth.

MAKING TURNS

The way a yacht turns is governed by four major factors:

1 The size, shape and position of the keel relative to the propeller.

2 The size, shape and position of the rudder relative to the propeller.

3 'Prop walk' pulling the stern to one side. Most propellers have clockwise rotation in forward gear, which will pull the stern slightly to starboard. In reverse gear, anti-clockwise will pull the stern to port. The relationship between keel and propeller can create pronounced prop walk in reverse gear.

4 Wind blowing the boat off course. When a yacht is motoring slowly, particularly astern, the bows will be blown away from the wind by a strong breeze. If the wind is blowing onto the port side, the bows will swing to starboard.

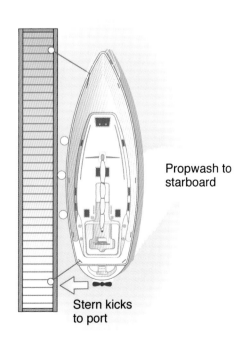

Propwash to starboard

Stern kicks to port

POWER TURNS

You need power to turn the boat. More power and the use of prop walk creates a faster, tighter turn. Motor forward at a steady speed. When you are ready to turn, pull the gearshift back into neutral. Immediately turn the rudder hard to starboard, so that the boat starts turning round its pivot point. Pull the gearshift into reverse gear and give a blast of throttle. Prop walk will drag the stern to port and accelerate the turn, which should be completed within seconds as the boat almost spins in its own length. With the wheel still hard to starboard, a quick burst of throttle ahead before returning to neutral will continue the turn without the boat gathering any momentum.

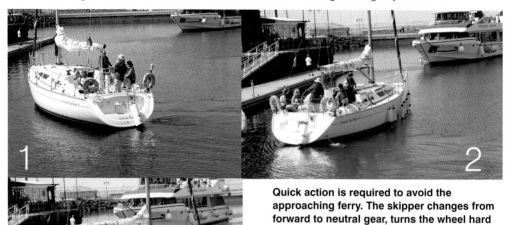

Quick action is required to avoid the approaching ferry. The skipper changes from forward to neutral gear, turns the wheel hard to starboard and gives a blast of throttle in reverse gear to drag the stern left while the boat keeps pivoting to starboard.

> **The yacht will heel over as it spins through the turn. Be sure to warn the crew before starting this dramatic manoeuvre.**

12 BOW THRUSTERS

Larger cruising yachts may have the luxury of bow thrusters, which shoot a jet of water out of the bow on the port or starboard side, indicated by red and green buttons on the binnacle control panel. Bow thrusters do not replace the rudder, since they have limited effect on changing the course of a yacht with a large keel. However, bow thrusters can be very helpful for assisting you in manoeuvring in tight spaces – particularly with wind on your beam.

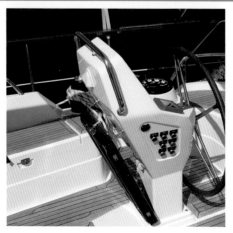

Buttons for port and starboard bow thrusters next to the wheel on a luxuriously equipped Nauticat 351, which has 5 more buttons for electric sheet winches, plus mainsail and headsail furling!

REVERSING

Most modern cruising yachts handle well when reversing. Some older yachts, particularly with full length keels, can be a total nightmare astern. Whatever kind of yacht you are handling, experience through practice will make reversing a lot more relaxed!

■ The main challenge when reversing is to maintain steerage. You will need some speed – typically 2–3 knots minimum – to keep the boat tracking in a straight line. Speed is necessary to overcome the effects of prop walk dragging the stern to one side and the wind blowing the bows off course.

■ Keep rudder movements small – no more than 10 degrees to either side. If you push the rudder over too far, it will act like a barn door and spin the boat. This is particularly important for maintaining control when reversing with a tiller.

■ Take a long run when reversing into a tight berth. This will give enough time to get proper steerage and ensure the boat is heading in the correct direction. If prop walk is dragging the stern to one side, change to neutral gear for a few seconds.

■ Keep enough speed to maintain a flow of water over the rudder, which will steer the boat.

■ Stop the boat by changing to forward gear with a burst of throttle. It may be a wise precaution to put a large fender across the stern.

■ You are driving backwards, so face aft and look where you are going!

Take a long run when reversing into a tight berth and look behind you!

FENDERS

- Use at least three fenders to protect the widest part of the boat. Tie each fender to the guardrails with a clove hitch. This will make it easy to slide each fender along the guardrails and adjust the height to get a perfect position.
- When leaving or entering a tight berth, one crew can stand by with a 'roving fender'. This can be dropped over the side, when fending off from another yacht.
- If you are reversing into a berth, hang a large balloon-shaped fender off the stern. Alternatively, tie a large sausage fender horizontally across the stern.
- Pay particular attention to the height the fenders are placed at – just above the water for a pontoon or level with the toe rail if rafting alongside another boat.

When leaving or entering a tight berth, one crew can stand by with a 'roving fender'.

FENDING OFF

Beware of fending off with hands or feet, which could get crushed between the gap. For safety, always use a roving fender. Keep young children well away from the danger area when coming alongside.

COMING ALONGSIDE

- When coming alongside a pontoon, you will need bow and stern lines to secure the yacht to pontoon cleats.
- Attach the end of the stern line to a mooring cleat on the stern of the yacht. Either take several turns round the cleat, or tie a bowline through the centre hole. Lead the coil of rope through the fairlead in the toerail, then lift the coil back over the top of the pushpit into the cockpit. This will ensure that the stern line has a direct lead to the dock. Use the same technique to prepare the bow line.
- Approach the dock at the slowest possible speed required to maintain steerage. Remember that a yacht with a heavy keel will 'carry its way' and keep moving for some distance when you shift into neutral gear. If the yacht is moving too fast, shift into reverse gear and use a burst of throttle to bring it to a halt.
- Wait until the yacht is alongside before stepping ashore with the bow and stern lines. Do not attempt to leap from the yacht to the pontoon, which could be dangerous. The crew with the bow line should move aft to the shrouds, where the yacht is widest and it is easiest to step ashore. Use your engine to ensure the vessel is stopped before it touches the pontoon alongside.
- Be prepared to 'snub' the yacht and hold it alongside with the bow and stern line. Take one turn round the cleat as quickly as possible and be ready to put on more turns to hold the weight. Never try to pull against the yacht without using a cleat.
- Wait for the yacht to settle down, with the bow line led to a cleat just ahead of the bows and the stern line led to a cleat just behind the stern. Adjust the bow and stern lines so the yacht lies parallel alongside, then attach springs to prevent the yacht moving forward or back. For instance, the ends of both springs could be attached to

1 The helm aims the bow towards the dock, then turns the wheel to make the boat pivot round the mast to pull the stern in.

2 One crew steps carefully onto the dock with the bow warp. Do not get off the boat unless you are confident it is safe.

3 One crew steps carefully onto the dock with the stern warp. Stepping from the side deck, where the boat is widest, makes it easier to get ashore.

4 Both crew take a turn round the dock cleats to hold the yacht. Never pull against the power of a boat without a holding turn.

Securely moored alongside. Bow and stern lines are secured by bowlines and led back to cleats on deck. Stern and bow springs are tied to a cleat halfway along the dock.

12

a cleat mid-way along the pontoon. The bow spring is led forward to a cleat on the bows of the yacht and the stern spring is led aft to a cleat on the stern of the yacht. The term 'spring' is because they act like springs, stretching a little and then easing

back whenever the yacht moves.
- If the stern is adjacent to a pontoon, use an additional stern line on the 'outside' to hold the transom at right angles, which looks tidier and makes it a lot easier to get on and off the boat.

DIFFERENT APPROACHES

- Use wind to your advantage. Make your final approach to a berth while heading bows-first into the wind, which will help to stop the boat when you come alongside. Get the bow line onto a pontoon cleat first to prevent the bows being blown out. If your final approach is with wind behind, the boat will be driven on by the wind when you come alongside. Get the stern line onto a pontoon cleat first to prevent the stern being blown out.
- The effect of tide is often stronger than wind, since it is running around the hull and keel. When possible, make your final approach into the tide.

Approach no wind – use prop walk

If the boat is not affected by wind or tide, aim for the dock and use prop walk to pull in the stern.

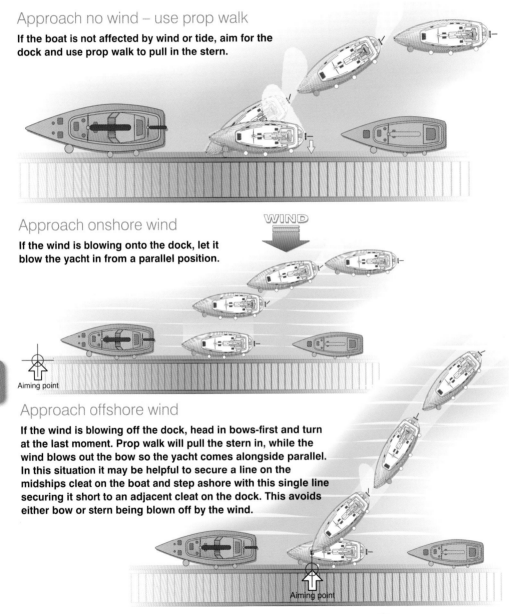

Approach onshore wind

If the wind is blowing onto the dock, let it blow the yacht in from a parallel position.

Approach offshore wind

If the wind is blowing off the dock, head in bows-first and turn at the last moment. Prop walk will pull the stern in, while the wind blows out the bow so the yacht comes alongside parallel. In this situation it may be helpful to secure a line on the midships cleat on the boat and step ashore with this single line securing it short to an adjacent cleat on the dock. This avoids either bow or stern being blown off by the wind.

Approach into stream

When tide is stronger than wind, approach bows-first into the tidal stream, which will help to push in the stern.

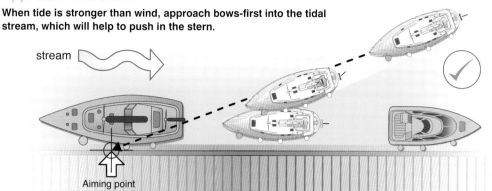

Berthing with a stream

If you have to approach with the tide, stop adjacent to the berth and reverse ferry glide into your desired position.

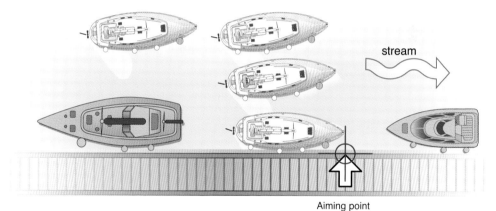

Ferry gliding

Motoring slowly ahead at a slight angle to the tidal stream, which hits one side of the bows and pushes the boat in.

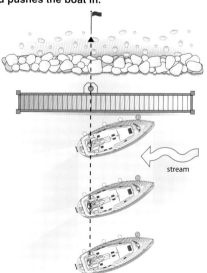

Reversing into a marina berth. The bows will swing in as the helm turns the wheel to the right, bringing the yacht neatly parallel alongside the pontoon.

EXIT STRATEGIES

When leaving a marina berth, you have the advantage of being able to assess the situation by walking round the dock. Ideally, you can also choose your departure time to suit wind and tide, or wait for neighbouring boats to leave their berths. Do not rush into casting off your mooring ropes – careful planning always helps ensure a stress-free departure! In simple situations you can just motor away from a berth. But if you are lying alongside, the stern will get kicked in towards the dock as you try to turn away. For this reason, many exit strategies rely on the use of springs.

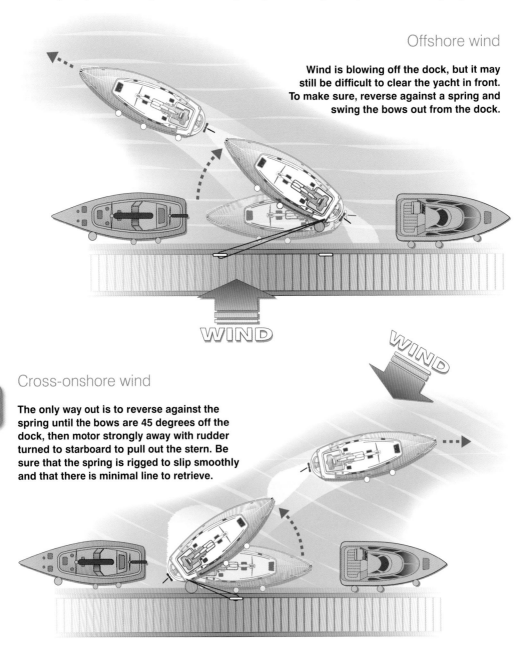

Offshore wind

Wind is blowing off the dock, but it may still be difficult to clear the yacht in front. To make sure, reverse against a spring and swing the bows out from the dock.

Cross-onshore wind

The only way out is to reverse against the spring until the bows are 45 degrees off the dock, then motor strongly away with rudder turned to starboard to pull out the stern. Be sure that the spring is rigged to slip smoothly and that there is minimal line to retrieve.

12

Full onshore wind

It is not always possible to leave bow-first without being blown onto the yacht in front, unless you can get the bow pointing almost towards the wind. Instead, motor ahead against a spring to swing the stern out from the dock. The bow will tend to be blown downwind as you reverse away from the dock.

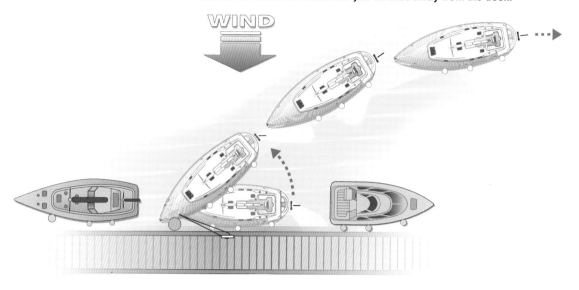

Onshore wind against pontoon

If you reverse straight out, the yacht will drag alongside the pontoon and the bow will crash against the end. Motor ahead against a spring to swing the stern out from the pontoon, then reverse strongly away whilst slipping the spring.

12

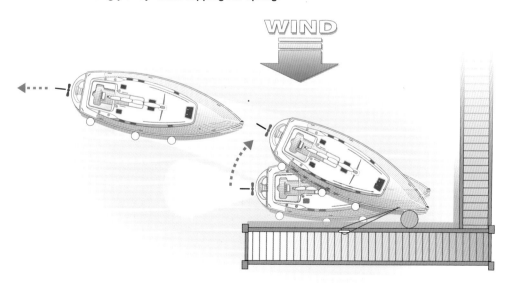

Pulling out of a tight berth

Using a spring will not pull the bow or stern far enough out to avoid the surrounding boats. Take a line across to the pontoon and pull the bows round until the yacht can motor straight ahead.

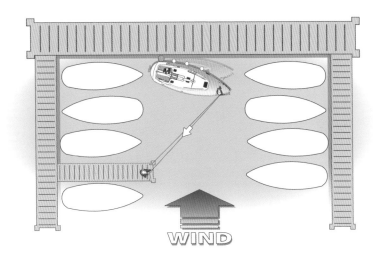

Leaving a raft

When an inside yacht wishes to leave, the outside yacht must be attached to the dock at the non-exit end of the raft (bows in this example). A loose rope is attached to the dock at the exit end of the raft (stern) and will be passed to the outside yacht as the inside yacht leaves. The crew can quickly pull in the bow and stern lines to rejoin the raft.

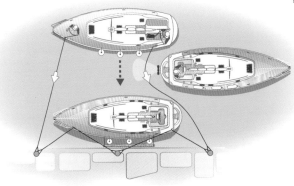

Exit stern-first into tide

Motor ahead against a spring to swing out the stern, which will be swept out by the tidal stream, then reverse away.

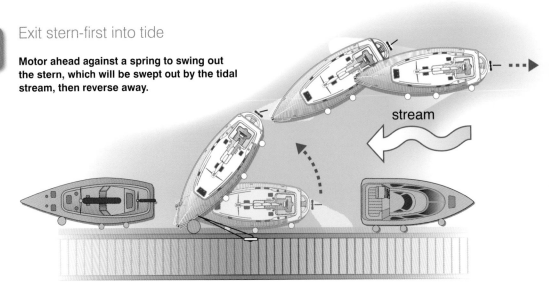

stream

12

A simple departure with light wind blowing the yacht off the pontoon. Be ready to make a 90 degree turn out of the marina berth, using engine power to swing the stern outwards and ensure the bows pivot round. In some marinas, particularly in the Mediterranean, there is very little space between lines of moored boats. Put one crew on the bow to signal when the bows are close, then spin the wheel and use plenty of power to pivot the yacht through 90 degrees, being sure your stern is clear of the vessel alongside. It is well worth practising this manoeuvre, building up confidence performing tight turns inside a marina without any danger of ramming other boats!

Exit bows-first into tide

Motor astern against a spring to swing out the bows, which will be swept out by the tidal stream, then power ahead.

12

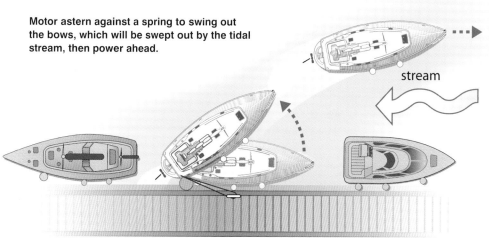

stream

USING A MID-SHIP SPRING

Some berthing manoeuvres are trickier than others. One manoeuvre that often challenges a skipper is to bring the boat alongside a pontoon when the wind is blowing you off and you have very few crew. The use of a mid-ship spring can make your life much easier in this situation. Prepare a warp that is led through a fairlead at mid-ships, ensuring you have a large loop with both ends attached to the boat at either a mid-ship cleat or led aft to a winch. The loop needs to be large enough for a crew member to drop over the cleat on the pontoon but not so big as to allow the vessel to drift too far from the pontoon.

Approach the pontoon either ahead or in astern and get your vessel as close to the pontoon as possible, using your throttle to stop the boat when in position. Have a crew member standing at your mid-ship point ready to drop the loop over the cleat.

Once the boat is secured via the spring it can blow only as far off the pontoon as the spring will allow. This is very useful when you are being blown off by a strong wind and means you do not have to endanger your crew by having them step off a moving boat.

1 Make your approach either stern first or bow first using only as much throttle as you need to maintain steerage.

2 As you draw alongside, have a crew member drop a loop of mooring warp over the cleat. Ensure both ends of the warp are secured to the boat. Use just enough throttle to stop the boat.

3 Allow the boat to settle as the wind blows the boat and tensions the spring.

4 Motor ahead slowly using the engine to drive against the spring. Bring the boat gently to rest alongside the pontoon. You can now step off and secure all lines.

This is a wonderful technique for safely making contact and securing alongside a pontoon when shorthanded, or when being blown away from a pontoon.

12

SPRINGING OFF

Motoring ahead against a simple bow spring (with warps taken off) forces the stern away from the dock. Use a large balloon fender or two standard fenders to provide a cushion between the bow and the dock. Once the stern is well away from the dock, take in the spring and reverse away. Conversely, motor astern against a stern spring to push the bows away from the dock.

Always take a turn round a cleat when holding a boat on a bow/stern line or spring.

RAFTING-UP

On occasions you may need to raft alongside other yachts. The yachts are connected by bow-to-bow and stern-to-stern lines, with springs to prevent fore and aft movement and plenty of fenders between the boats. Spreaders should not overlap, helping to prevent potential damage if the yachts start to roll. Outside yachts should ideally have separate lines led direct to the dock.

12

MEDITERRANEAN BERTHING

The normal style in Mediterranean marinas and harbours is to berth stern-to a dock, without finger pontoons between the yachts.

The classic method is to drop the anchor and reverse up to the dock, while paying out the anchor chain. You then attach the yacht to the dock with two stern lines at 45 degree angles and tension the anchor chain. There are three problems. Firstly, you may lay your anchor chain across the chain of another yacht or vice-versa. Secondly, your anchor may get jammed under old cables or anchors on the sea bed. Thirdly, it can be very difficult estimating when to drop the anchor in a strange harbour. If you drop too soon, you will not reach the dock. If you drop too late, the anchor chain will be too short to hold the bows securely.

Because of all these difficulties, many Mediterranean marinas use the more sophisticated lazy line method:

1. Put fenders on both sides and a large fender low down on the stern.
2. Prepare two stern lines.
3. Reverse up to the dock, taking a long approach with enough speed to ensure the yacht goes straight astern.

4. Wait until the stern is within three metres of the dock before shifting into neutral. Use forward gear to slow the boat if necessary.
5. The yacht will continue moving back, allowing two crew to step ashore with the stern lines when the yacht is half a metre from the dock.
6. They must take turns round cleats or bollards on the dock without any delay. At that point, shift gently into forward gear to hold the stern off the dock.
7. You will see a lightweight line attached to the dock, emerging from the water on the starboard side of the stern, which is the lazy line for your berth. One of your shore crew must pick up that line, bring it aboard and walk it forward along the side deck.
8. The lazy line is connected to the end of a heavy duty mooring rope, which will be connected to something like a concrete block on the harbour bottom 10 metres or more in front of the bows of your yacht. When you have pulled up the end, which may be covered with rather disgusting weed, pull it in through the bow roller or starboard-side fairlead and drop the loop over the main cleat on your foredeck.

9. Adjust the stern lines and mooring rope so the yacht is held tight at 90 degrees to the dock. You may need to rig a mooring warp to the bow line or, alternatively, shorten up the bow line to ensure your yacht is correctly positioned relative to the pontoon.

Leaving a berth with a lazy line requires a little care:

1. Start the engine and rig stern lines for 'slipping' to ensure an easy getaway. Remember that you must be able to let go the short end.
2. Let the mooring rope go from the bow whilst slipping the stern lines at the same time.
3. Engage engine slow ahead and guide the boat out of the berth, having a crew member walk the lazy line down the side of the boat as you depart.

Do not make the mistake of letting go the stern lines with the mooring rope still attached to the bows. It will drag the yacht forward and may be difficult to get off the foredeck cleat.

STERN-TO OR BOWS-ON?

- In Mediterranean marinas, it is normal to berth stern first. The advantage is that you can get on and off the boat very easily with the aid of a gang-plank. The disadvantage is lack of privacy when there are hordes of passers-by on the dock.
- Berthing bows-on works equally well with an anchor or lazy line. The approach to the berth is easier in forward gear and it is normally also easy to reverse out of your berth. However, getting ashore via the pulpit may be difficult.
- In some situations, it may be impossible to berth stern-to. For instance, very shallow water or underwater boulders next to the dock could damage your rudder, making bows-on berthing a safer option.

12

READ A BOOK

RYA Introduction to Boat Handling for Sail & Power (G68) by Rob Gibson **Comprehensive guide to handling a yacht under power including all you need to know about manoeuvres, marinas and moorings.**

13 SETTING SAIL

Sailing a yacht is all about balance. For optimum performance and maximum enjoyment, the sails must be balanced and working in harmony with the hull, keel and rudder. This is achieved by trimming the sails correctly and setting the correct amount of sail area for prevailing conditions.

BALANCING MAINSAIL AND HEADSAIL

The vast majority of modern yachts have a Bermudan sloop rig, with a single mast supporting a mainsail and headsail.

Variations are used to achieve a balanced rig.

■ The top of the headsail reaches the top of the mast on a masthead rig, allowing more sail area forward of the mast.

■ The top of the headsail reaches part-way up the mast on a fractional rig, allowing more sail area aft of the mast.

13

The Bavaria 32 rig is nicely balanced with jib and reefed mainsail in a fresh breeze. In addition, the high clew of the small jib provides the crew with excellent visibility to leeward.

VARIATIONS ON A BALANCED RIG

Traditional and classic yachts achieve balance by means that are seldom found on modern yachts, frequently due to cost and complexity. However, the end result should always be the same, with a lightly balanced rudder providing just a touch of weather helm to make it as easy as possible to steer the yacht.

CUTTERS AND YAWLS The magnificent yawl to leeward has a mizzen mast and sail to counter-balance her mainsail and two headsails. The equally magnificent cutter rigged sloop to windward has a relatively larger mainsail balanced by a jib and inner staysail. Two smaller headsails are more easily managed than one very large headsail, but the yacht may not point so well to windward with the inner sail backwinding.

MASTHEAD RIG A large masthead genoa overlapping the shrouds, balanced by a smaller mainsail, was the most popular solution for best sailing or racing performance with a well-balanced rudder during the 1960s. The popular Kim Holman-designed Twister shown here has one reef in the mainsail balanced by a few rolls in the genoa.

GAFF CUTTERS The gaff cutter *Kismet* designed by William Fife is rigged with an extremely long, heavy wooden boom and shorter (but still heavy) gaff to support the mainsail, with extra sailpower provided by the inverted topsail, two headsails and a large spinnaker. The effect is magnificent, with a great deal of expense and expertise required to create a well-balanced yacht.

CAT RIG The unusual cat rig is occasionally used by modern designers, including David Thomas who designed the sweet-handling Liberty 22. Both masts are unstayed with mainsail well forward balanced by slightly smaller mizzen and no headsails. This rig is extremely simple and easy to manage with particularly good performance on a reach compromised by less good performance beating upwind or running downwind.

BALANCING WITH A BOWSPRIT
Grace is a replica Essex fishing smack built in concrete. The long bowsprit balances the mainsail and topsail, which ensures she is sweet on the helm. Without the bowsprit, her bows would pivot into wind due to having far too much sail power over the stern.

13

UNDERWATER BALANCE

The weight and shape of the keel holds this Bavaria 32 upright, prevents it being blown sideways and converts sail power into forward motion.

The keel of a yacht has three major functions. First, its heavy lead weight provides a counter-balance to the sails, ensuring the yacht cannot capsize like a dinghy.

Second, the keel helps prevent the yacht being blown sideways by the wind in the sails, known as leeway.

Third, the foiled shape of the keel helps transform power in the sails into forward drive.

HEELING OVER

A modern yacht is designed to heel at no more than 10–20 degrees. If it heels further, the keel will lose grip and the yacht will begin to slip sideways. The yacht will also slow down, due to having less power in the sails and the side of the hull pushing down into the water, which increases drag. The most important side effect will be increased weather helm. As the angle of heel increases, the yacht will develop a natural tendency to turn towards the wind, which becomes difficult to control.

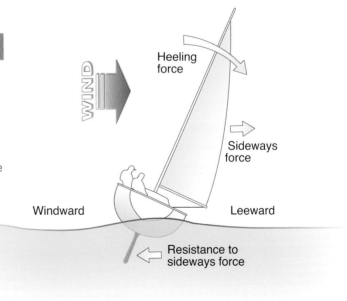

WIND

Heeling force

Sideways force

Windward

Leeward

Resistance to sideways force

13

DIFFERENT HEADSAILS

■ A jib has a short foot and long leech. The clew is forward of the shrouds when fully sheeted in on a beat. Typically it has a narrow high aspect shape. The advantage is easy handling, particularly during tacks.

■ A genoa has a long foot, which creates a much bigger sail. The clew is aft of the shrouds and overlaps the mainsail when fully sheeted on a beat. The advantage is maximum power, but there can be a lot of sail area for the crew to wind in.

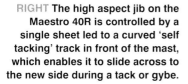

RIGHT **The high aspect jib on the Maestro 40R is controlled by a single sheet led to a curved 'self tacking' track in front of the mast, which enables it to slide across to the new side during a tack or gybe.**

The genoa overlaps both mast and mainsail on the Broadblue 38.

13

BALANCING RUDDER AND SAILS

A well balanced boat should always feel light on the helm, with just a slight tendency to turn towards the wind. This 'weather helm' should make the steering feel pleasantly responsive with a hard edge, but must never feel heavy or difficult to control.

'Lee helm' is a tendency to bear away from the wind, which is not relaxing at all. Neutral helm has a dead feeling, which provides minimal sailing pleasure. It is most likely to be due to an unresponsive steering mechanism.

Excess weather helm indicates too much power in the mainsail or too little power in the headsail.

If you start battling with the wheel to prevent the yacht turning towards the wind, it's time to reef the mainsail, or at the very least to de-power it by easing the boom vang and/or mainsheet.

SOLUTIONS:
1. Easing the mainsail provides a temporary solution in a gust.
2. Reefing the mainsail provides a permanent solution in stronger winds.
3. Sheeting in the headsail may help if the sail is under-trimmed. Check that telltales are flying on both sides of the sail.

Excess lee helm indicates too much power in the headsail or too little power in the mainsail.

SOLUTIONS:
1. Easing the headsail provides a temporary solution in a gust.
2. Reefing the headsail provides a permanent solution in stronger winds.
3. Sheeting in the mainsail may help if the sail is under-trimmed.

13

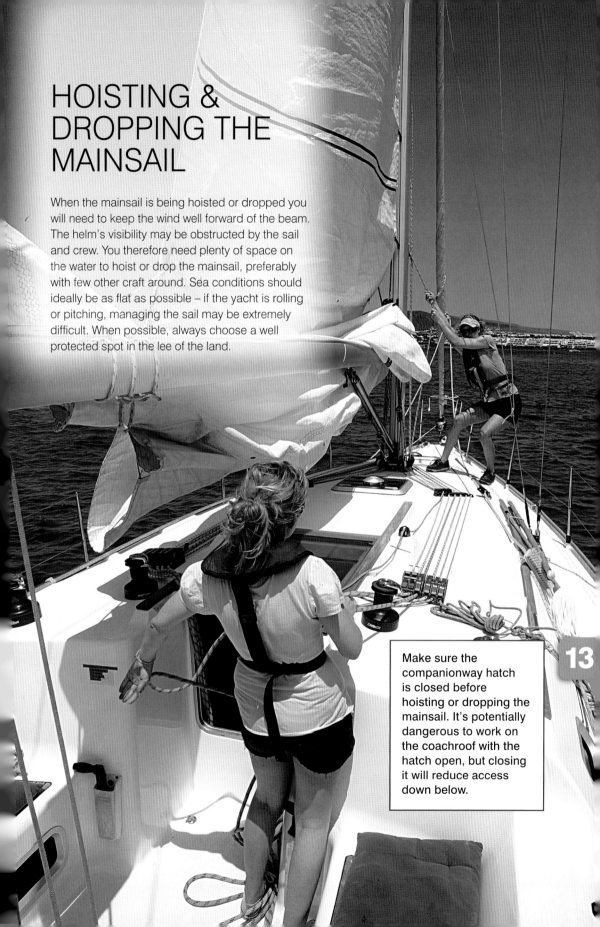

HOISTING & DROPPING THE MAINSAIL

When the mainsail is being hoisted or dropped you will need to keep the wind well forward of the beam. The helm's visibility may be obstructed by the sail and crew. You therefore need plenty of space on the water to hoist or drop the mainsail, preferably with few other craft around. Sea conditions should ideally be as flat as possible – if the yacht is rolling or pitching, managing the sail may be extremely difficult. When possible, always choose a well protected spot in the lee of the land.

Make sure the companionway hatch is closed before hoisting or dropping the mainsail. It's potentially dangerous to work on the coachroof with the hatch open, but closing it will reduce access down below.

13

MAINSAIL WITH STACK-PACK AND LAZY JACKS

If the mainsail has a network of lazy jack lines and a stack-pack along the boom, all you need do is ensure the main halyard is attached, unzip the stack-pack and pull up the mainsail. There is one big disadvantage with this system. When you hoist, the ends of battens in the leech have an incredible ability to get snagged under lazy jack lines. You must keep the yacht pointing very precisely into the wind so the sail is centred between the lazy jack lines while it is hoisted. This is not so easy on a breezy day. When a batten end snags, you must ease off the halyard to let the sail drop until the batten is free, then hoist again. Remember to ease off the vang, reefing lines and mainsheet before starting to hoist.

Snagging on lazy jack lines is less of a problem when you drop the mainsail, but the helm still needs to focus on keeping the yacht pointing into wind with the sail centralised. The great thing about this system is that most of the sail will fall inside the stack-pack. However, the crew will need to pull the last two or three metres of luff down the mast and bundle excess sail into the stack-pack before doing up the full length zip.

HOISTING

1 It is fastest to pull the halyard down at the mast and take up the slack from the cockpit when you start pulling up the sail.

2 To ensure the sail does not snag on lazy jacks, the helm should motor slowly forward and steer to keep the sail in line with the boom.

3 With most of the sail hoisted by hand, the cockpit crew will wind up the remainder with the winch as the load on the halyard increases.

13

LOWERING

1 If the sliders run easily, the mainsail will drop as soon as you let go the halyard. The boom must be at the right angle to catch the sail inside the stack pack.

2 One crew will need to move onto the coach-roof to pull down the head of the mainsail and secure the halyard. The mainsheet must be pulled in tight to prevent the boom moving.

IN-MAST FURLING

Some cruising yachts have in-mast furling, which allows the mainsail to roll up inside the mast. In theory, this is a really neat system. The mainsail can be rolled out or rolled away in seconds, or partly rolled to provide the most suitable size of sail. However, a furling mainsail cannot be fitted with horizontal battens to support the leech and is consequently limited to a triangular pin-head kind of shape. Even when fitted with diagonal battens, the performance of a furling mainsail will not match a conventional mainsail and will deteriorate when it is rolled to a smaller size. My own experience is that pulling a rope on the coachroof to roll or unroll the mainsail is not quite so easy as it sounds, plus there is the slight worry that one day the furling mechanism might jam!

13

MAINSAIL WITH TRADITIONAL SAIL TIES

If there are no lazy jack lines and stack-pack, sail ties will be used to hold the mainsail in a tight bundle on top of the boom.

■ When you are ready to hoist the sail, work along the boom undoing the sail ties. Sail ties can be stowed on the binnacle with a simple overhand knot, ready for immediate use. Alternatively, the hand-holds on either side of the companionway are useful for stowing sail ties.

■ With no sail ties to hold it in position, the mainsail will flop down off the boom and obscure the helm's vision. This makes it important to pick a clear area for hoists and drops and manage the sail as quickly as possible.

■ When hoisting or dropping the mainsail, the helm will need to keep the yacht heading towards the wind, but there will be considerably more latitude than with lazy jacks.

■ Dropping a mainsail without lazy jacks is labour intensive. At least two crew will need to work on the coachroof alongside the boom. Pull down the luff as tightly as possible. Then use concertina-folds to lay the mainsail along the top of the boom, pulling the leech back to make each fold

With no stack-pack, sail ties are used to secure the folded sail on top of the boom.

neat and tidy. Use sail ties to secure the folded sail on top of the boom. While this is going on, the helm's view may be severely restricted.

■ When the mainsail is tied onto the boom with the main halyard attached to the head, a good tip is to lead the halyard under the sail tie closest to the mast. This will hold the head down and prevent the sail rising up the mast, while ensuring it can be hoisted with minimal delay.

KEEPING HEAD TO WIND

In most situations, the helm will need to motor gently ahead to keep the yacht pointing into wind while the mainsail is hoisted or dropped, with just enough speed to prevent the bows being blown off course. Do not go any faster than necessary – minimum speed will be best for the crew. It normally suffices to keep the engine in slow ahead, with occasional short bursts in forward gear to prevent the bows blowing offwind.

13

TOPPING LIFT

The topping lift is a rope that holds the end of the boom up when it is not supported by the mainsail. This is very important – never risk dropping the boom on a crew member's head.

- The topping lift is attached by a snap-shackle to the end of the boom. From there it is led to the top of the mast, then down to a cleat near the base of the mast.
- Before the mainsail is lowered, the topping lift must be tensioned to support the weight of the boom and hold it horizontal.
- When the mainsail is hoisted, the topping lift will need to be eased off to allow the sail to be sheeted in tight when beating upwind. Some skippers will choose to remove the topping lift from the end of the boom and secure it to the base of the mast while sailing, but for cruising the topping lift can invariably be left attached to the boom.

MAINSHEET

- Before hoisting the mainsail, you will need to uncoil the mainsheet and let it run free. Be aware that with no mainsheet tension, the boom can flop from side to side. This is potentially dangerous for anyone sticking their heads up or moving along the decks.

- Before dropping the mainsail, you will need to uncleat the mainsheet to let the sail flap from side to side as it comes down onto the boom. Then tension the mainsheet, which will be pulling against the topping lift, so that the boom is steady enough for the crew to pack away the sail.

SAIL CONTROLS

- Release the clutch for the kicking strap (boom vang) before hoisting the mainsail. There may also be a cunningham (downhaul) control line, which must also run free.
- If you are hoisting full mainsail without any reefs, make sure the reefing clutches are all open. If you are hoisting a reefed sail, make sure the appropriate reefing pennants for first or second reef are locked down. Reefing pennants have a lot of friction. A pennant may get stuck where it passes through a clutch, through a stainless steel cringle in the leech of the sail, or where it exits from the end of the boom. It may help to pull the pennant through by hand, but be very careful if you are stretching up trying to loosen pennants on the leech. Check that the mainsheet is secure and make sure the helm steers a steady course to keep the boom in a fixed position.

13

TIME TO HOIST

- Stand in the cockpit and pull in slack on the main halyard, with two clockwise turns round the winch and the clutch closed.
- The quickest way to get the mainsail up is for the crew to 'sweat up the halyard'. One crew stands by the mast and pulls down the halyard hand-over-hand, with the cockpit crew pulling in the slack round the winch. When the mainsail is past halfway, the halyard may start to get heavy. The mast crew uses a 'down and out' movement to pull a length of halyard away from the mast, which the cockpit crew immediately takes in on the winch. When there is too much weight to pull any more halyard at the mast, the cockpit crew takes two more turns round the winch and locks the rope in the jaws of the self-tailing mechanism in order to wind the mainsail to the top of the mast.
- If you prefer not to 'sweat up the halyard', the cockpit crew can simply pull and wind the halyard all the way up the mast. It may appear simpler, but tends to be slower and actually requires more physical effort.
- Sometimes, it will seem very difficult to pull or wind the mainsail up the mast. The normal culprit is reefing pennants holding

1 Pass the sail ties to the cockpit crew who will stow them for future use. It can be convenient to loop them around the binnacle or companionway handles.

down the leech, but also check that the mainsheet and boom vang are running free.
- For good performance, it is vital to get a tight luff on the mainsail with no sag between the sliders. Apart from winding the halyard up as tight as possible, the yacht may be fitted with a cunningham line to provide downward tension on the luff.
- Once the leech is tight, tension the kicking strap (boom vang), which is used to

2 For a fast hoist, the deck crew pulls the halyard at the mast with the cockpit crew pulling in slack by the winch.

3 Use a 'sweating' technique, pulling the halyard down and out and back in as the cockpit crew pulls in slack.

13

4 When the sail is more than three-quarters up, the halyard will become too heavy to pull by hand – now it is time to use the winch.

5 Winding up the mainsail on a self-tailing winch is surprisingly slow! Keep winding until the luff above the boom looks really tight.

hold the boom down when the mainsheet is eased for sailing offwind. Ease off the topping lift, which is used to hold up the boom without the sail, until it is slack enough to pull the mainsheet tight when sailing upwind. The end of the topping lift may be led down to a cleat on the side of the mast or back to a jamming cleat on the coachroof, so it can be eased or tensioned from the cockpit.

6 Having finished hoisting the mainsail, tension the boom vang (kicker) which is used to hold down the boom.

TIDYING UP

With the main halyard securely locked by its clutch, take the rope off the winch and coil it neatly. Make sure the halyard will not turn into spaghetti when dropping the mainsail – it must be able to run free when you let go.

To prevent unused reefing pennants flapping around, pull them back until almost taut, then close the clutches. The ends of all these ropes should be coiled neatly, so they are ready for use and will not get tangled. A useful solution is to drop ropes down the companionway, but make sure they are separate, tidy and not on the floor.

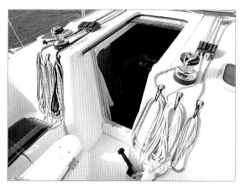

This is the neatest way to tidy up excess rope, but when sailing it may be easiest to drop the coils down the companionway.

13

DROPPING THE MAINSAIL

1 With no stack-pack, you need to be prepared to catch the mainsail. One crew stands ready to pull down on the luff when the halyard is let off.

2 The sail is 'flaked' in concertina folds along the top of the boom, which must be sheeted tightly for security while the crew works on the exposed coachroof.

3 Gather up folds and pull them back along the boom as neatly as possible. During this time, the helm will not be able to see ahead.

4 Use reef knots to secure short lengths of rope used as sail ties. Short lengths of webbing with a loop in one end are easier to tension and tie – take a turn round the loop and secure with a simple slip knot. Shock-cord elastic sail ties can be dangerous if you let go under tension.

13

TRIMMING THE MAINSHEET

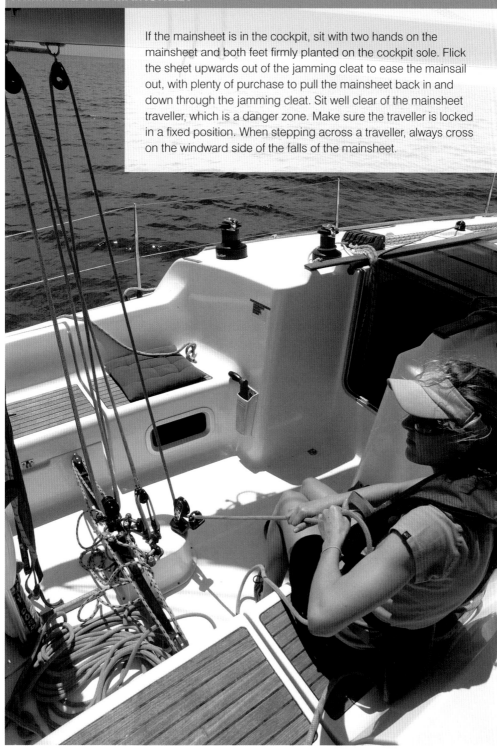

If the mainsheet is in the cockpit, sit with two hands on the mainsheet and both feet firmly planted on the cockpit sole. Flick the sheet upwards out of the jamming cleat to ease the mainsail out, with plenty of purchase to pull the mainsheet back in and down through the jamming cleat. Sit well clear of the mainsheet traveller, which is a danger zone. Make sure the traveller is locked in a fixed position. When stepping across a traveller, always cross on the windward side of the falls of the mainsheet.

13

OPERATING A FURLING HEADSAIL

Most cruising yachts have furling headsails which roll and unroll around the forestay.

If you unlock the furling line and pull on the leeward sheet, the headsail will roll out with a bang as the wind takes control! This is not a good idea. The crew should always keep control when you unfurl the headsail by keeping a couple of turns of the furling line around a nearby winch and easing the sail out.

Primary winches for headsail and spinnaker sheets are often sited on the cockpit coamings, which means you may have to lean over and wind in an uncomfortable position. Primary winches on the coachroof can provide plenty of space for two crew to work in a fairly comfortable position, well clear of the mainsheet and traveller.

Motor-sailing with the mainsail on a beam reaching course is ideal for unfurling the headsail, which will blow away from the boat and be partially blanketed by the mainsail as it unrolls.

UNROLLING THE HEADSAIL

- Let off the windward headsail sheet so it will run free.
- Crew No1 should take two clockwise turns round the primary winch with the leeward headsail sheet and pull in to take out any slack.
- Crew No2 should take two turns round a secondary winch with the furling line, hold the free end tightly and pull up the lever to open the furling line clutch.
- Crew No1 pulls the headsail sheet in with both hands, while Crew No2 eases the furling line – pulling on tension and closing the clutch will stop the headsail unfurling.
- At first, the headsail will unfurl slowly as the sheet is steadily pulled in. But as the sail gets bigger, it will start to unroll faster and faster.
- The stronger the wind, the more quickly the headsail will power up and unroll, which is when the furling line is used to maintain control.

13

ROLLING UP THE HEADSAIL

Make sure the furling line clutch is locked down in the closed position. In very light winds, you may be able to ease off the leeward headsail sheet and pull the furling line in hand-over-hand. If there is any load on the furling line, take two clockwise turns round a winch and pull in by hand. If the load gets very heavy, you can take extra turns and wind the furling line in, which is a slow but sure method.

When pulling in on the furling line, keep slight tension on one or both headsail sheets. This will help to ensure that the sail rolls up as tightly as possible. Keep rolling until the clew rolls around the sail, then pull back and cleat both sheets to hold the roll in position.

Furlex electric furling at the base of the forestay on a luxurious Nauticat 351. No furling line is required – just press a button to furl or unfurl the headsail!

Pull the furling line to unroll the drum and furl the headsail. Keep light tension on the sheets to ensure the sail rolls up tightly.

REEFING THE SAILS

'Reefing' is reducing sail area to prevent the yacht from being overpowered in stronger winds. When a yacht is sailing upwind or on a reach, it will heel to leeward as pressure increases on the sails. Heeling at an angle of about 10–15 degrees should provide optimum performance, but performance will start to decline if the yacht heels much further.

At an angle of 30 degrees, when the toerail gets close to the water, the yacht will make excessive leeway (sliding sideways) as the keel loses traction. The rudder will feel heavy and unbalanced, due to excess weather helm. The crew will need to brace with their feet while sitting in the cockpit and find it difficult to move around down below. The mainsheet may need to be eased to prevent the side deck disappearing under water each time there is a heavy gust. You will know it is time to reef the sails!

Depending on the relationship between the length and weight of the keel, shape and buoyancy of the hull and size of the rig, the behaviour of a yacht under sail will range from 'tender' to 'stiff'. A tender yacht will heel easily and reefing will become necessary in a moderate Force 3–4 breeze. A stiff yacht will stay upright for longer and it may only be necessary to reef in a strong Force 5–6. Most modern cruising yachts attempt to compromise between providing good performance in lighter winds and reasonable stiffness in stronger winds.

Running downwind with 2 reefs and small jib on a Finngulf 41. It looks untidy, but that flat mainsail will work extremely well in strong winds.

13

WHICH SAIL DO YOU REEF FIRST?

A well designed cruising yacht should be perfectly balanced with full sail in a light to moderate breeze. It should track straight on a reach or sailing upwind, with just a hint of weather helm providing feedback to the helmsman. When you reduce sail area, it is important to preserve the correct balance between the sails. Too much power in the mainsail will produce heavy weather helm and make the yacht turn towards the wind. Too much power in the headsail will produce

lee helm and make the yacht turn away from the wind. As a general rule, given that it is easier to depower the mainsail using the sheet than it is the headsail, it is a good idea to reduce sail area by partially furling the headsail first, then putting a reef in the main. If working with a non-furling headsail a sudden increase in wind will see the need to drop the headsail quite quickly.

REEFING SAILS

The ratio of mainsail area to headsail area should stay in the same ball park when you reef the sails. For instance, one slab reef in a mainsail could be balanced by furling 33% of a genoa.

■ Most cruising yachts have slab reefing systems for the mainsail. This produces an efficient sail shape with one, two or three reefs, due to equal amounts of sail being pulled down on the luff and leech.

■ Most cruising yachts have roller furling systems for the headsail. This is extremely convenient, but does not produce an efficient sail shape with a partly rolled sail, since the foot will tend to sag and balloon as the sail gets smaller. Hoisting a smaller headsail such as a number 3 jib will always provide better performance, particularly when sailing upwind.

REEFING A MAINSAIL – SLAB REEFING

Unless a yacht is fitted with in-mast furling, slab reefing is the standard method of reducing the size of the mainsail. Colour coded 'reefing pennants' (control lines) identify the first, second or third reef. Each reef removes a horizontal 'slab' from the sail. The mainsail may be fitted with single reefing pennants, which pull down the leech, or double reefing pennants, which pull down both the leech and luff.

PULLING DOWN REEFS

You will normally need to be sailing towards the wind, in order to put in a reef. If you are sailing downwind, with the sail pressed against the shrouds, it will be difficult to pull the reef down and tension the sail. The same procedure is used for 1st, 2nd or 3rd reefs.

1. Check there is sufficient topping lift tension before lowering the sail.
2. Place the boat on a close reach and sailing on the head sail.

3. Open the clutch for the kicking strap so it will run free.
4. Ease off the mainsheet.
5. Prepare to lower the main halyard. Take two or three turns clockwise round the winch, insert the handle and wind it in just a fraction. This will take tension off the clutch and allow you to flip up the handle.
6. Ease the halyard to bring the mainsail down to the appropriate reefing point.

SINGLE REEFING PENNANTS

With single reefing pennants, one crew will need to work on deck.

1. One crew stands on the coachroof by the mast. As the halyard is lowered by the cockpit crew, pull the sliders physically down the mast until you can grab the reefing cringle or ring. (If there are 3 reefs in the sail, there will be 3 reefing cringles on the luff at the same height as 3 reefing pennants passing through 3 reefing cringles on the leech.)

2. Pull the reefing cringle down onto the stainless steel reefing hook by the side of the boom. Hold it there until you are sure it cannot slip off.
3. The cockpit crew wind in the halyard until the shortened luff is taut.
4. To complete the reef, the cockpit crew put the correctly coloured reefing pennant (1st, 2nd or 3rd reef) on a winch, make sure the clutch is closed and wind it in. Keep winding until the cringle in the leech is pulled tightly down onto the boom.

5. Ease the topping lift.
6. Re-trim the mainsail and tension the kicking strap.

The cockpit crew lowers the main halyard, enabling the foredeck crew to pull the reefing cringle ring down over the hook on the boom end, after which the halyard is wound back up to re-tension the luff of the mainsail.

13

DOUBLE REEFING PENNANTS

With double reefing, the reefing pennants for leech and luff are led back to the cockpit on either side of the companionway, so there is no need to go on deck.

1. Lower the main halyard to allow for the reef.
2. Put the coloured reefing pennant (for 1st, 2nd or 3rd reef) for the luff on a winch, make sure the clutch is closed and wind it in until the luff cringle is pulled down onto the boom.
3. Wind in the halyard until the shortened luff is taut against the mast.
4. To complete the reef, put the correctly coloured reefing pennant (1st, 2nd or 3rd reef) for the leech on a winch, make sure the clutch is closed and wind it in. Keep winding until the cringle in the leech is pulled tightly down onto the boom.
5. Adjust the topping lift.
6. Trim the mainsheet and then re-tension the kicking strap.

TAKING OUT REEFS

Reverse the procedure to take out reefs. The yacht should be between a close reach and close hauled, sailing on the headsail.

1. Let off the mainsheet and kicking strap.
2. Tension the topping lift.
3. Let off the pennant which is holding the reef in the leech. Make sure the clutch is fully open and the pennant runs free.
4a. If the mainsail has a single reefing pennant, ease the main halyard and slip the reefing cringle off the hook, standing next to the mast.
4b. If the mainsail has a double reefing pennant, let off the pennant which is holding the reef in the luff.
5. Wind up the halyard until the luff is taut.
6. Adjust the topping lift.
7. Trim the mainsheet and then re-tension the kicking strap.

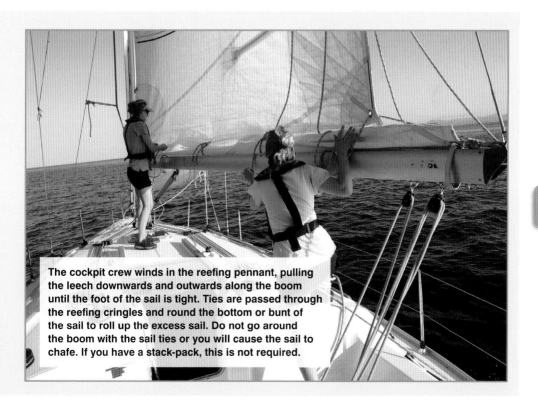

The cockpit crew winds in the reefing pennant, pulling the leech downwards and outwards along the boom until the foot of the sail is tight. Ties are passed through the reefing cringles and round the bottom or bunt of the sail to roll up the excess sail. Do not go around the boom with the sail ties or you will cause the sail to chafe. If you have a stack-pack, this is not required.

13

HEADSAIL ROLLER REEFING

Most cruising yachts make do with one headsail for all wind strengths. The exception is storm force, when you may have the option of changing to a storm jib or surviving without any headsail.

Take two or three clockwise turns round a winch and pull in by hand.

Reefing the headsail uses exactly the same techniques as rolling it away.

1. Make sure the furling line clutch is locked down in the closed position.

2. Ease the leeward headsail sheet.

3. Take two or three clockwise turns round a winch and pull in by hand. If the load gets heavy, take extra turns and wind the furling line in with the winch handle.

4. Keep rolling until the sail is sufficiently reduced in size.

5. Move the headsail sheet traveller cars forward to allow for a shorter foot.

6. Sheet in and see what the sail looks like! It will have more belly at the front and the yacht will not be able to point so high to windward.

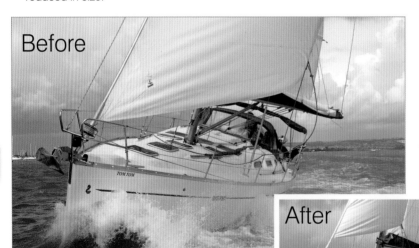

Before

After

The sail will have more belly at the front and the yacht will not be able to point so high to windward.

13

CHANGING HEADSAILS

Furling headsails are convenient and user-friendly, but have one major disadvantage. Sail efficiency goes progressively downhill as you roll the sail to smaller sizes. A more efficient solution is to carry two different sized headsails – one large and one smaller:

- Genoa for light to moderate winds.
- High aspect 'blade' jib with a short foot for moderate to strong winds.

Either sail can be furled round the forestay when not in use. Changing is likely to be easiest in a marina, but can also be done on the water.

1. Fully unfurl the sail.
2. Let off the headsail halyard and pull the sail down the luff groove on the forestay.
3. Gather the sail on deck inside the guardrails.
4. Undo the sheets at the clew and tie them together.
5. Unclip the tack. Unclip the halyard from the head and temporarily clip it to the pulpit.
6. Roll or flake the sail and put it in a bag.
7. Feed the top of the bolt rope of the new headsail into the luff groove. Feed it through a 'guide' if fitted.
8. Attach sheets to the clew.
9. Clip on the tack and clip on the halyard.
10. Hoist the sail, feeding the bolt rope into the luff tube to help prevent it from jamming.
11. Tension the halyard until the luff is taut.
12. Adjust the headsail sheet traveller cars on both side decks. When sailing, the foot and leech of the headsail should be equally taut. You therefore need to move the cars forward when changing to a headsail with a shorter foot.

13

READ A BOOK

RYA Manual of Seamanship (E-G36)
by Tom Cunliffe

Comprehensive and practical hardback guide to all aspects of seamanship. Part of the RYA Yachtmaster series and essential reading for anyone taking RYA Day Skipper or RYA Yachtmaster.

14 HANDLING A YACHT UNDER SAIL

Sails need to be trimmed to provide maximum performance and ensure the boat is well balanced regardless of what point of sail you are on.

For optimum performance in a fresh breeze, the jib of this Bavaria 32 is sheeted tightly with the main sail sheeted close to the centreline. Wind accelerates through the slot between jib and mainsail, increasing performance when beating to windward.

BEATING TO WINDWARD

Many cruising yachts do not perform particularly well when beating to windward. The combination of a tubby hull to maximise accommodation, short keel for mooring in shallow water and underpowered rig for easy handling will not help the yacht to point high or sail fast like a racing yacht.

■ Unless the wind is very light, pull the mainsheet in reasonably tightly and make sure the traveller is close to the centre.

■ Use the primary winch to wind the headsail in tight until the leech is almost, but not quite, touching the shrouds.

Top and middle telltales are streaming nicely with the bottom telltale starting to lift, indicating good airflow across the leeward side of the jib.

Despite Force 6 winds, this Finngulf 41 felt beautifully light on the helm with a perfectly balanced sail plan helping to drive the yacht upwind.

HELMING

Steering with a wheel or tiller upwind requires concentration and sensitivity. Your objective is to keep the boat sailing as fast as possible while pointing as high as possible upwind.

■ Watch the Windex® on the top of the mast. The tail of the moving arrow should be more or less in line with the fixed arm of the Windex®. This will be replicated by electronic wind instruments in the cockpit.

■ Watch the telltales near the luff of the headsail. If they are all lifting on the windward side, you need to bear away to get them streaming. Alternatively, pull the sheet in tighter to flatten the headsail.

■ Watch the front of the mainsail between the mast and boom. If it is back winding you either need to sheet the main in further or alternatively bear away from the wind a fraction.

■ Does the rudder feel balanced or heavy? Can you sail with one hand? If it feels heavy, try easing the mainsheet to take power out of the mainsail. If that doesn't solve the problem, you probably need to take in a reef.

Typical wind instrument found on a well equipped yacht, which indicates the wind is coming from 30 degrees to starboard of the bow and we are making 6.32 knots.

14

HOW HIGH CAN YOU POINT UPWIND?

A cruising yacht may be able to point as high as 35 degrees to the wind, but an average of 50 degrees or lower is more likely. Pointing ability may be severely impaired with a partly-furled headsail or sailing into waves, which will stop the boat unless you bear away by a few degrees.

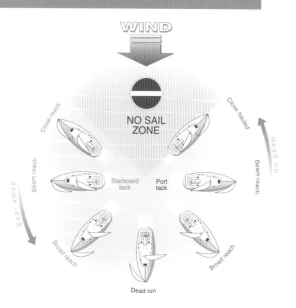

The helm has the Sun Fast 37 pointing high and footing fast, with a tight slot between mainsail and jib and all the telltales streaming.

SHEETING IN AND OUT

If the wind is variable, or the helm keeps changing course, you will need to trim the headsail to the correct angle.

To sheet in, use the winch handle to wind the sheet in on the self-tailing jaws.

To ease out, take the sheet out of the self-tailing jaws and ease until it slips round the winch, being careful to keep your hands well clear of the winch at all times. If there is too much friction, take another turn off the winch drum. Always keep fingers on the outside of the rope and away from the drum.

1 When easing off the sheet, keeping tension on the line, unwind the working end of the rope from the self-tailing jaws.

2 Keep tension on the working end and lead it round in a circle until the rope you are holding is parallel with the rope leaving the drum.

3 Hold the end of the rope taut and ease it out smoothly. If necessary use your left hand to 'palm' the coils carefully on the winch to assist them to slide.

HOW TO USE TELLTALES

Wind streams over both sides of a sail, creating high pressure on the windward side and low pressure on the leeward side, which pulls and sucks the sail.

- Telltales are lightweight streamers – sometimes known as 'woolies' – attached at different heights near the leading edge of a headsail. Sailing upwind, the windward telltales should be starting to stream slightly upwards, with the leeward telltales streaming back horizontally.
- If windward side telltales stop streaming, you either need to pull in the sheet or bear away. If leeward side telltales stop streaming, you either need to ease out the sheet or head up.

Telltales indicate airflow over both sides of the sail. For optimum performance they should be streaming back.

- Windward telltales provide instant feedback when sailing upwind or on a reach; leeward telltales will be slower to respond to changes in wind flow.
- There are normally two or three sets of telltales at different heights. They will not all stream perfectly in unison. Owing to sail twist (the leech of the sail is more open at the top), upper telltales may start to lift while lower telltales still stream aft. However lower telltales are most important, since they provide feedback on the sail area with maximum power.

Under-Trimming

Windward telltale higher

Correct Trim

Telltales fly parallel

14

Over-Trimming

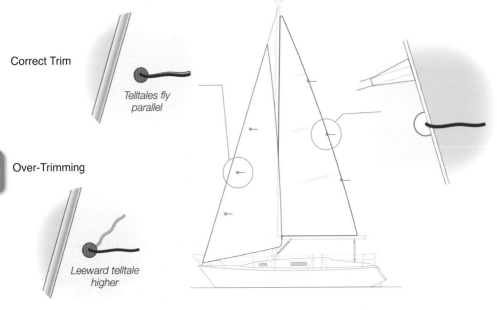

Leeward telltale higher

Broad reaching downwind on the Nauticat 351 with wind blowing from behind the beam at about 45 degrees to the stern.

REACHING ACROSS THE WIND

Reaching is the fastest and most comfortable point of sailing.

Close reach – wind ahead of the beam.
Beam reach – wind on the beam.
Broad reach – wind aft the beam.

- Ease the mainsheet until the mainsail is just inside the angle of the wind indicator. When sailing on a broad reach, keep the boom just off the shrouds. If the sail starts flapping, pull the boom in. It may be preferable to ease the mainsheet traveller to the leeward end of the track, then lock it in that position. The kicking strap must be tensioned to hold the boom down.
- Ease the headsail sheet until the headsail is almost parallel to the mainsail. Trim the sheet until telltales are streaming back on the windward side.
- Does the rudder feel balanced or heavy? Can you sail with one hand? If it feels heavy, try easing the mainsheet to take power out of the mainsail. Reefing the mainsail will be difficult with the boom out and the sail pressing against the shrouds. The easiest solution may be to bear away and sail on a broader reach – as the wind moves further behind, the boat will heel less and feel more comfortable.

SPINNING PROPELLER

The propeller shaft will tend to spin when you are sailing with the engine turned off, even with a folding propeller. This makes an annoying noise and increases wear on the bearings. Pull the control lever back into reverse gear to lock the prop shaft. Remember to push the lever into neutral before starting the engine.

14

RUNNING WITH THE WIND

Running directly downwind on a classic 12 Metre America's Cup yacht with the wind blowing from behind.

Running straight downwind with the jib goose-winged on the opposite side to the mainsail.

Sailing with the wind blowing from directly behind is not as fast or as relaxing as you might expect. You cannot outrun the wind and there is only pressure on one side of the sails, which reduces power and limits speed. The yacht will not heel over, but heeling against the wind helps provide stability on a beat or a reach. There is no lateral stability when running downwind, so the yacht may roll from side to side.

Ease the mainsail all the way out, then pull the mainsheet back a fraction to prevent the boom pushing hard against the shrouds. Make sure the kicking strap is pulled down to hold the boom horizontal.

Ease the headsail sheet until the headsail is almost parallel to the mainsail. The problem is that the headsail will be 'blanketed' by the mainsail when running downwind.

There are two solutions:

1. Sheet in the headsail on the windward side. This is 'goosewinging' with one sail on each side of the mast. You will need to rig a spinnaker pole between the clew of the jib and the mast to keep the headsail filled – this is known as poling out. You will also need to rig a 'preventer' between the end of the boom and the bow to prevent the mainsail from gybing across on this point of sail. Helming downwind requires a greater level of experience and concentration.

2. Head up onto a broad reach so the headsail is unobstructed by the mainsail.

14

BEWARE GYBE

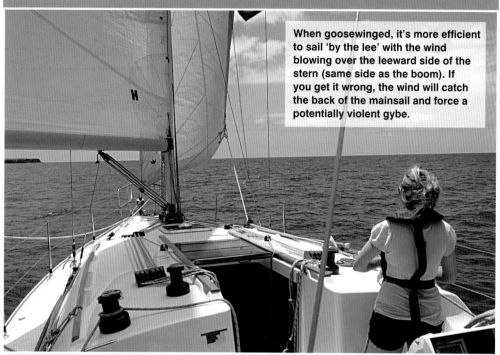

When goosewinged, it's more efficient to sail 'by the lee' with the wind blowing over the leeward side of the stern (same side as the boom). If you get it wrong, the wind will catch the back of the mainsail and force a potentially violent gybe.

Sailing directly downwind puts you in the 'gybe zone'. If you steer too far to leeward, which can easily happen if the stern of the yacht is pushed to windward by a passing wave, wind pressure will hit the back of the mainsail and force it to gybe. An uncontrolled gybe is potentially dangerous, with the boom unexpectedly whistling across the cockpit at high speed. Preventative action should include:

1. Only allow the most experienced crew to steer when running downwind in a following sea.
2. Do not allow crew on deck. Warn them to keep low in the cockpit and keep clear of the falls of the mainsheet.
3. Use a 'preventer'. Attach a strong rope to the end of the boom, lead it forward through the bow fairlead and back to a cleat, forming the widest possible triangle between boom and preventer. The object is to restrain the boom if the helm steers too far to leeward and provide enough time to correct course to windward, without an unexpected gybe. However, if the yacht makes a big turn to leeward, the preventer may not be able to restrain the power of the sail.

Another option is to change course to windward. A broad reach is much more stable than a dead run. There is less danger of gybing, the yacht will not roll downwind and will sail faster. In some situations, it is a lot more pleasant to gybe from broad reach to broad reach on a downwind course.

Use a preventer to restrain the boom.

FLYING A CRUISING CHUTE

A cruising chute provides a lot of extra power for this Hunter Legend 340. The tack is secured to the stem by a short strop, with the working sheet led back to the cockpit. You can just see the snuffer immediately above the pink triangle at the top of the cruising chute, below the radar reflector attached to the front of the mast.

14

A cruising chute is an asymmetric shaped spinnaker, which is most effective on a broad reach. It can also be flown when running directly downwind, but will need to be held out by a pole on the windward side. The chute is attached to a cleat on the bows with a tack line. For trimming, two sheets are led to turning blocks and winches close to the stern.

- A spinnaker halyard is used to pull the chute up the mast inside a 'snuffer sock' fitted with a plastic mouth at the bottom. When it is time to launch, a continuous line is used to pull the plastic mouth up to the head of the sail, allowing the chute to gradually fill with wind.

- When it's time to drop the chute, pull the sock all the way down to 'snuff out' the sail. Then let go the halyard and lower the filled sock onto the foredeck or down through the forehatch. It is a wise precaution to ensure the mainsail blankets the chute to prevent it blowing out of control, when pulling the sock up or down in a fresh breeze.

- Keep steering on a broad reach with a cruising chute. If you steer to windward, the wind will swing from the stern to the beam and apparent wind will increase. The result is that you may suddenly get a lot more power in the sail, which makes the yacht heel over. If the yacht heels right over, the rudder will lose its grip on the water and the yacht will turn further into the wind and push more power into the chute. To avoid this, you should bear away and ease the sheet if the yacht starts heeling at more than 15 degrees or so.

- For maximum drive, the cruising chute should be as full as possible. For perfect trim, ease out the sheet until the luff starts to curl inwards, then pull the sheet back in a fraction. If the chute keeps collapsing, experiment with bearing away or heading up to fill the sail.

USING A SPINNAKER

A symmetrical spinnaker is a multi-purpose downwind sail, which is particularly effective on a dead run, but also works well on a broad reach. It is also a complex and demanding sail, which is not recommended for use by inexperienced crew and is beyond the scope of this book. Here are a few tips:

- The spinnaker must be supported by a spinnaker pole between the mast and clew on the windward side.

- A 'guy' (rope used as the spinnaker sheet on the windward side) controls the horizontal angle of the pole, which is pulled back at approximately 90 degrees for running dead downwind and can be let forward as far as the forestay (but never pressing against the forestay) for when the wind is coming from further forward.

- A sheet (used as the spinnaker guy on the other tack) is used to trim the spinnaker.

- Uphaul and downhaul lines control the vertical angle of the pole, which can also slide up or down the mast on a track. This allows the two corners of the spinnaker to fly at the same height on all points of sailing, which helps keep the spinnaker balanced and under control.

14

Having the main hoisted can help steady the yacht when motoring, so long as the sail is partly filled by apparent wind on one side.

MOTORSAILING

Most cruising yachts sail very slowly in light winds, particularly when beating to windward. Using the engine at moderate revs will help drive the boat forward and create apparent wind. It will enable you to point higher towards the wind, with the added benefit of charging batteries and pumping cold air around the fridge!

■ Using the engine at moderate revs will also help drive the boat to windward and get through waves in strong winds, when you are making slow progress under sail alone. It is advisable generally when motor sailing to furl away the headsail – remember also to bear away enough to ensure your mainsail is not flogging.

■ If it is flat calm, you can motor without any sails. If there is swell, apparent wind flowing over the mainsail may help to 'stiffen' the yacht and prevent rolling.

■ A black cone should be hoisted to make clear to other craft that you are motoring under sail. You have the same rights as other powercraft and should give way to sail.

TACKING

You will need to sail a zig-zag course to sail directly towards the wind, tacking from port to starboard or vice versa. Before starting a tack, the yacht needs to be sailing at good speed on a beating course close to the wind, ensuring that it will turn smartly onto the new course. The mainsheet can stay cleated throughout the manoeuvre.

1. The helm says "Prepare to tack".
2. Crew No1 gets ready to let off the sheet which is holding the sail in on the leeward side. The sheet is removed from the self-tailing jaws and held by hand.
3. Crew No2 gets ready to pull in the other headsail sheet on the new leeward side, putting three turns clockwise round the winch and pulling in the slack.
4. The helm says "Ready about?" and the crew reply "Ready".
5. The helm turns the vessel towards the

wind calling "Lee ho" when the working headsail sheet should be released.

6. The crew should wait until the headsail begins to backwind before letting off the headsail sheet. This will let wind blow back against the headsail and push the bows through the remainder of the tack.
7. When letting off the sheet, ease it round the drum, then use an upward movement to spin the rope off the winch.
8. Pull in the sheet as quickly as possible before the headsail starts to fill on the new side. When the load gets heavy, take another turn around the winch and pull the sheet into the self-tailing jaws. Put the winch handle carefully into the top of the winch and wind the headsail in until the sail is properly trimmed, then remove the winch handle from the winch.
9. The helm adjusts course for the new tack.

1 Tacking from a beat on starboard to a beat on port tack: "Ready about?" The crew replies "Ready," the helm turns towards the wind and calls "Lee ho" when he is ready for the headsail sheet to be released.

2 One crew lets off the headsail sheet as the bows turn through the eye of the wind. The other crew starts pulling in the headsail sheet on the new side.

3 As the helm bears away to get up speed on port tack, the crew winds in the headsail until it is fully sheeted.

4 Having accelerated up to speed, the helm turns the wheel to point as high as possible towards the wind.

14

GYBING

Gybing is used to change tacks from port to starboard or vice versa when sailing downwind. Unlike a tack, when the wind is blowing from ahead, the wind is blowing directly onto the mainsail from behind the boat. This means the mainsail is fully powered throughout the manoeuvre. Consequently the boom can crash from side to side, which makes gybing a potentially dangerous manoeuvre. A controlled gybe will prevent any problems:

1. The helm says "Prepare to gybe".
2. The crew pull in the mainsheet hand-over-hand until the boom is right above the cockpit, ensuring it can only swing through a tightly restricted arc during the gybe.
3. The crew prepare to let off the headsail sheet and pull in the sheet on the new side.
4. The helm says "Ready to gybe?" and the crew reply "Ready".
5. The helm calls "Gybe-ho" and turns the wheel or pulls the tiller to turn the boat away from the wind and onto the new course.
6. As the stern passes through the eye of the wind, the boom will swing to the new side. The helm bears away onto a broad reach before straightening the rudder. Beware of letting the yacht turn too far into the wind, which will make it heel over with too much power in the rig. Keep your gybing angle narrow and the yacht will stay as controlled and upright as is possible.
7. As soon as the boom has gybed, uncleat the mainsheet and ease the boom all the way out for a deep downwind course on the new gybe.
8. Let go the old headsail sheet and pull in on the new side. The sheet does not need to be tight for sailing downwind, so you should be able to pull it in by hand with three turns round the winch.

The helm adjusts course for the new gybe.

1 Gybing from a run on starboard to a run on port tack: "Ready to gybe?" The crew starts to wind in the mainsail.

2 With the mainsail wound to the centreline, the crew says "Ready," the helm says "Gybe-ho!" and bears away into the gybe.

3 As the stern turns, the wind catches the outside of the mainsail and forces it to gybe to the new side. The controlled arc makes this as risk-free as possible.

4 The crew eases out the mainsheet while the helm concentrates on steering downwind on the new gybe.

14

GYBING WITH A SPINNAKER

Gybing with a cruising chute is simple. As soon as the boom has swung across to the new side, let the sheet right off. The cruising chute will blow round the front of the forestay and can then be sheeted in on the new side.

Gybing with a symmetric spinnaker is not simple. Firstly, the spinnaker pole has to change sides. Secondly, you have to keep control of the spinnaker with two free-floating corners during the gybe. Various techniques are used to gybe the pole – it can be unclipped from the guy, unclipped from the mast, clipped on to the new guy and then reattached to the mast at the opposite end of the pole. During this 'end-to-end' manoeuvre, both ends are temporarily detached from both the guy and the mast whilst the middle of the pole is supported by the crew and topping lift. Another option is 'dipping the pole'. The end is unclipped, the pole is dipped between the forestay and mast, and swung across to be clipped onto the new side. Both methods require plenty of practice in light winds and an experienced helm who can steer the unsupported spinnaker carefully through the gybe.

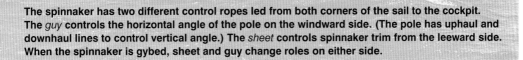

The spinnaker has two different control ropes led from both corners of the sail to the cockpit. The *guy* controls the horizontal angle of the pole on the windward side. (The pole has uphaul and downhaul lines to control vertical angle.) The *sheet* controls spinnaker trim from the leeward side. When the spinnaker is gybed, sheet and guy change roles on either side.

TAKE A COURSE

Sign up for an RYA practical yachting course from novice to advanced level. There is also a great range of shorebased RYA theory courses available.

RYA Start Yachting

A short introduction to sailing for complete beginners.

Pre-course experience: None

Minimum duration: 2 days.

Content: The yacht, ropework, under way, rules of the road, man overboard recovery, clothing and equipment, emergency equipment and precautions, meteorology.

RYA Competent Crew

This course is for beginners and those who would like to become active crew members rather than just passengers.

Pre-course experience: None

Minimum duration: 5 days. Often run over 3 weekends or 3 days plus a weekend.

Content: Knowledge of sea terms and parts of a boat, rigging and sails, sail handling, ropework, fire precautions and fighting, personal safety equipment, man overboard, emergency equipment, meteorology, seasickness, helmsmanship, general duties, manners and customs, rules of the road, dinghies.

14

RYA Day Skipper Practical

A course for aspiring skippers with some yachting experience and basic navigation and sailing skills.

Pre-course experience: 5 days, 100 miles, 4 night hours on a sailing yacht. Basic knowledge of navigation and helmsmanship. RYA Day Skipper shore-based course certificate is recommended.

Minimum duration: 5 days, 3 weekends or 3 days plus two days.

Content: Preparation for sea, deck work, navigation, pilotage, meteorology, rules of the road, maintenance and repair work, engines, victualling, emergency situations, yacht handling under power, yacht handling under sail, passage making, night cruising.

RYA Coastal Skipper

Advanced skippering techniques for yachtsmen and women with considerable knowledge of sailing and navigation wanting to undertake coastal passages by day or night.

Pre-course experience: 15 days on board, 2 days as skipper, 300 miles, 8 night hours. Boat handling to the standard of RYA Day Skipper and navigation to shorebased RYA Coastal Skipper / RYA Yachtmaster Offshore course level.

Minimum duration: 5 days.

Content: Passage planning, preparation for sea, pilotage, passage making and ability as skipper, yacht handling under power and sail, adverse weather conditions and dealing with emergencies.

RYA Yachtmaster Coastal and RYA Yachtmaster Offshore Certificates of Competence

Having gained all the theory knowledge and gone on to get some significant practical experience you may wish to sit an exam to gain your RYA Yachtmaster certificate of competence. These qualifications are a mark of great personal achievement and can also be commercially endorsed for use as qualifications within the marine industry.

14

15 ANCHORING & MOORING

There is nothing better than dropping the anchor or picking up a mooring buoy in a beautiful location, but you need to be absolutely sure the yacht is secure, particularly for an overnight stay.

THE PERFECT ANCHORAGE

An anchorage should provide:

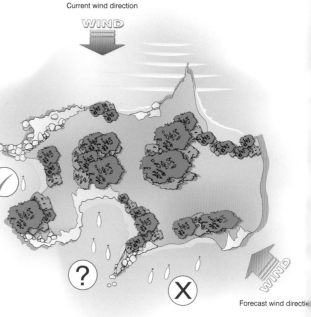

Current wind direction

Forecast wind directi◄

1. Shelter from all directions

A typical 'perfect anchorage' might be a horseshoe-shaped bay encircled by cliffs or hills, ensuring good shelter from all wind directions, unless it is blowing straight through the entrance which would drive in swell and make the bay extremely uncomfortable. Be aware that wind often swings through 180 degrees during the night, when a strong sea breeze changes to a light land breeze. Anchoring in the lee of high hills or mountains may appear to provide the best possible shelter, but not when a katabatic wind (from the Greek word katabatikos meaning 'going downhill') accelerates down the hillside at violent speed!

2. Flat water

Ideally, your anchorage should be as flat as a mill-pond. Any swell will make it extremely uncomfortable. If the yacht starts rolling, things seldom get better. Best advice is to move on as soon as possible to seek an

Anchored in a deep Turkish bay with a stern line attached to the shore to prevent the yacht swinging.

15

A yacht should have room to swing through a 360 degree arc, without hitting anything under or on top of the water.

alternative anchorage. This may be caused by the wind swinging onshore. However, swell is unpredictable and can roll in during the night if you are unlucky. The best solution is departure at dawn.

3. Good holding
Anchors are incredibly effective at holding a yacht, but need good holding. The best surfaces are sand or mud, which allow the anchor to dig in deeply. Rock and weed or shingle will provide less secure holding. Never drop an anchor on coral.

4. Room to swing
A yacht should have room to swing through a 360 degree arc, without hitting anything under or on top of the water, including nearby yachts. All boats will swing as the wind or tide changes, though yachts and powercraft tend to swing at a different speed. If there is insufficient space to swing through a wide

arc or full circle, the solution may be to attach a stern line to the shore, which will hold the yacht in a fixed direction. This is useful when there is limited space in an anchorage and common practice in Baltic countries such as Sweden and Finland.

5. Tidal effects
If you anchor in a tidal area, you need to be sure there will be enough water under the keel at low tide. The exception is if you wish to 'dry out' with a bilge keel yacht, lifting keel yacht or shallow draught catamaran. Tidal flow may also affect where you can anchor in a river or estuary. Every six hours, the yacht will swing through 180 degrees as the tide changes. An anchorage with the bows facing into wind and tide should provide flat water and good shelter for the crew in the cockpit, but the yacht may start to rock and the cockpit may get draughty when wind blows against the tide.

15

HOW MUCH WARP OR CHAIN?

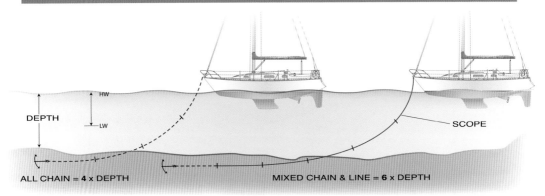

DEPTH

HW

LW

SCOPE

ALL CHAIN = **4** x DEPTH

MIXED CHAIN & LINE = **6** x DEPTH

- Secure holding requires sufficient 'scope' on the anchor warp or chain, which needs to lay out along the bottom, before rising to meet the yacht at an approximate angle of 45 degrees.
- The warp or chain is usually measured in either metres or feet. Let out enough scope for the maximum depth of water at high tide, using the following as minimum guidelines:
  4 x maximum depth for chain.
  6 x maximum depth for warp and chain.
- Heavy chain will provide greater security than warp, but puts a lot of weight into the bows and may be difficult to let go or pull up by hand.

Heavy chain may be difficult to pull up by hand. Care is required.

PARTS OF AN ANCHOR

SHANK – the main arm or stem of the anchor.

FLUKE – the holding part of the anchor buried on the seabed.

STOCK – cross-bar used to flip an anchor so the fluke digs into the seabed.

CROWN – where shank and fluke are connected.

TRIPPING RING – for breaking the anchor out with a tripping line.

15

LETTING GO THE ANCHOR WITH A WINDLASS

> *Anchors and chains are potentially dangerous. Wear gloves and sensible footwear. Keep fingers and hands away from a moving chain.*

An electric windlass uses a lot of power. The engine must be running, with the red button pushed in to engage neutral and the throttle lever pushed forward to provide sufficient revs. There is a particularly high load when pulling up a heavy anchor chain. Allow at least 1800 revs. If there is insufficient power, the electric supply may 'trip' and turn off. Make sure you know where the trip switch is located – normally low down behind the companionway – to flick the power back on.

The electric windlass is usually controlled by a hand unit, normally stored in the anchor locker or forecabin, which can be hand-held on the foredeck. The 'down' button winds the chain out; the 'up' button winds the chain in.

The electric windlass is controlled by a hand unit.

MANAGING THE BOW ROLLER

Most cruising yachts have the anchor stowed on the bow roller, so it is ready to drop. If the anchor is stowed in the anchor locker or on deck, you will need to lift it through the pulpit and onto the bow roller, which can be surprisingly difficult with a heavy anchor.

Make sure the lid of the anchor locker is held back by a safety leash, so it cannot blow shut. The anchor may be secured by a pin or lashing to ensure it cannot jump off the bow rollers or disappear over the side when the yacht is under way. Remove the pin or lashing to prepare for dropping. It may be necessary to let out a small length of chain on the winch and physically push the anchor forward on the bow roller, before gravity will allow it to drop.

15

Coloured markers or paint show how much chain has been dropped.

MAKE SURE THE END OF THE WARP OR CHAIN IS SECURELY ATTACHED TO THE YACHT. IT IS EMBARRASSING AND INCONVENIENT TO LET THE WHOLE LOT GO OVER THE SIDE!

MAKING THE DROP

The yacht should be facing into wind or tide – whichever is stronger – when the anchor is dropped. The yacht must also have stopped or be starting to move backwards as the anchor hits the water. It is a common mistake to drop when the yacht is still moving slowly forwards, which will lay out anchor and chain behind the yacht!

■ The skipper watches the depth sounder and instructs the crew when to drop by saying "Let go!" Press the down button to let the anchor chain run. The winch will let out a specific length per second – refer to the handbook – which can be used to control how much chain is let out.

■ The chain should lay in a straight line along the sea bed. You should let the yacht blow back with the wind or drift back with the tide, but it can be more effective to engage reverse gear and motor back from the anchor. Getting this right requires experience. The anchor must have a chance to dig in rather than being dragged along the bottom. It may

Turn the winch handle anti-clockwise to let the windlass run.

be necessary to drop the chain at much faster speed. Easing off the manual lock on the side or top of the windlass will let the chain run. It goes without saying that you must keep hands and feet well away from a moving chain.

■ When you have dropped sufficient scope, it is time to see if the anchor is holding. Give a burst of throttle in reverse gear. If the yacht pulls up short, the anchor is holding. If it keeps moving backwards, the anchor is dragging. The normal solution is to pull the anchor back up, choose a new spot and try anchoring again.

15

Make sure there are sufficient engine revs to keep lifting the chain.

Secure the anchor and close the chain locker lid.

PULLING UP THE ANCHOR WITH A WINDLASS

- Remember to keep the engine running in neutral with plenty of revs. If there is a lot of heavy chain, the windlass may need a rest. Press the 'up' button for 20 seconds, pause for 10 seconds, 'up' for another 30 seconds and so on.

- The chain will lift easily if it is vertical and pull hard if it is at 45 degrees to the bow. Let the weight of the chain pull the yacht forward until the chain drops straight down, before resuming the lift. You can use your engine to move forward over the anchor if you need to.

- The chain should disappear through the hawse pipe and fall down into the anchor locker below, but may occasionally jam. Keep your finger well away from the 'up' button when unjamming the chain.

- When the anchor 'breaks out' of the seabed, it will come up rapidly. Tell the helm as soon as this happens – you will either see the anchor approach the surface or feel the bows start to blow off to one side.

- Beware of the anchor damaging the bows when it breaks the surface. Keep lifting until it is in the bow roller, then secure with the pin or lashing.

15

TRIPPING THE ANCHOR

If there is a strong chance of the anchor getting stuck on the sea bed, possibly due to getting caught on rocks or beneath an underwater cable, try rigging a trip line. All you need is a reasonably strong line that is at least as long as the depth. Tie one end to the crown part of the anchor where shank and fluke are connected. Some anchors have a hole or tripping ring

for this purpose. Tie the other end to a small marker buoy, which could simply be an empty plastic container with a watertight cap. Throw out the marker buoy and line when you drop the anchor. If the anchor gets stuck, move the yacht close enough to grab the marker buoy with a boathook, then pull the trip line up hand-over-hand. The vertical pull on the fluke should help break out the anchor.

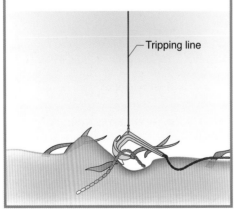

Tripping line

LETTING GO AND PULLING UP BY HAND

If there is no electric windlass, you will need to let go and pull the anchor up by hand. Heavy chain needs to be handled with extreme care. The skipper should have the engine running, ready to motor forward or astern if required.

■ Pull the chain up out of the anchor locker and flake it along the deck in a series of loops, which will provide sufficient scope for the depth of water. This will ensure that the chain runs free.
■ Before lowering, take a single turn of the chain round the nearest deck cleat to ensure you can hold the weight – extra turns will quickly lock the chain.
■ Let out the chain steadily hand-over-hand. Letting the chain run at full speed over the bow roller could be dangerous.

Chain is heav For security, pay out the chain with a turn round the deck clea when lowerin the anchor.

15

LEFT: Pull the anchor back into the bow roller and cleat the chain.

RIGHT: Choose a secure position when handling the anchor. Wear gloves and shoes!

15

You need back-up to pull up the anchor and chain. Instruct the helm to motor gently ahead to put slack in the chain. Be ready to take a turn round the deck cleat if it starts to pull. The crew with the boathook will retrieve the plastic bottle attached to the tripping line.

VEERING AROUND

If you are in a gusty anchorage, the bows of the yacht will veer from side to side, stretching the anchor chain in one direction, falling back and letting the chain go slack, then stretching the chain in the other direction.

This can be unpleasant, particularly if you are trying to sleep in the forecabin and the anchor chain is making a horrible grinding noise. Use a rubber 'snubber' to take the shock out of the anchor chain. Clip one end to the chain, just below the bow roller, secure the other end to a strong deck cleat, then slacken the chain sufficiently so the snubber will absorb each shock when the bows are blown back by the wind. Alternatively, let out a length of anchor chain connected to a length of warp, which will provide enough stretch to absorb shocks.

Use a rubber 'snubber' to take the shock out of the anchor chain.

AT ANCHOR

Take bearings or a transit on fixed objects so you can check that the anchor is not dragging.

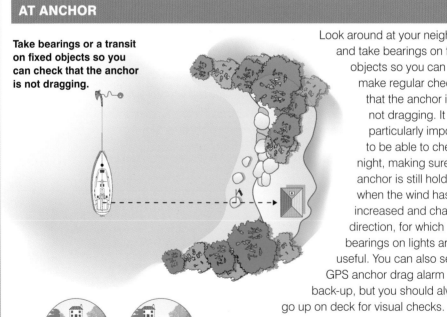

holding   dragging

Look around at your neighbours and take bearings on fixed objects so you can make regular checks that the anchor is not dragging. It is particularly important to be able to check at night, making sure the anchor is still holding when the wind has increased and changed direction, for which bearings on lights are useful. You can also set the GPS anchor drag alarm as back-up, but you should always go up on deck for visual checks.

■ Hoist the black anchor ball when at anchor.

■ If you are staying for the night, remember to turn the masthead anchor light on.

15

Approach very slowly with the bow to one side of the mooring buoy. The yacht should stop moving forward as soon as the buoy is within reach of a boathook.

PICKING UP AND DROPPING A MOORING BUOY

Choose a buoy laid for visiting yachts, which should hopefully be well maintained and secure. The maximum permitted length of yacht may be indicated on the buoy or in the local pilot book. It is also wise to check that tidal depth is sufficient for the draught of your yacht.

- Drop the mainsail and furl the headsail before approaching under engine directly into wind or tide, whichever is stronger.
- Make the final approach as slowly as possible, shifting to neutral in order to drift up and stop with the buoy close to one side of the bows. It is a common mistake to approach too fast and overshoot.
- A large mooring buoy may have a smaller pilot buoy floating alongside. Use the boathook to grab the pilot buoy and pull it onto the foredeck, either through the nearest fairlead or bow roller. The pilot buoy should be attached to a large mooring warp with a convenient loop to drop over the deck cleat, ensuring that the yacht is securely attached to the mooring. When it is time to leave, simply lift off the mooring rope, drop it in the water with

Once the yacht is securely attached, let out the mooring rope to drop back from the buoy.

the pilot buoy and allow the yacht to drop back, making sure the yacht is well clear of the mooring before motoring away.

- Alternatively, there may be a ring in the top of a large mooring buoy. Attach one end of a warp to a cleat, lead it through the nearest fairlead, round the mooring ring and back up to the fairlead and cleat on the opposite side of the bows. Reaching down and trying to get a rope round the buoy may be very difficult. A device such as the Bosco Boathook snaps onto the ring to provide a temporary mooring, while the crew get everything sorted, and can be released remotely for an easy getaway.

15

On a rough day, travelling by tender can be cold, wet and potentially dangerous if you fall out of the boat. Dress sensibly, take oars as a back-up if you use an outboard motor, make sure there is plenty of fuel and control your speed.

USING A TENDER

Whenever possible, row your tender! It's healthier, quieter and less of a hassle. Unfortunately, many modern yacht tenders are absolutely terrible to row, but you should always carry oars and practise in case the outboard lets you down.

Do not overload the tender. Maximum capacity should be clearly marked. It is sensible to wear lifejackets. Step into the middle of the tender before sitting down, preferably with weight on both sides. Alcohol and water don't mix – be sensible if using a tender after an evening out.

15

Sitting at the bows is not recommended if it's choppy – you will get wet!

It's easiest to get in and out of a tender from the transom platform, unless the stern is rising and falling on waves.

Secure the tender side-on to the stern for easy access and maximum stability getting on or off the boat.

USING AN OUTBOARD

To attach an outboard, you will need to secure the tender at right angles to the transom of the yacht, with painters holding the bow and stern. Lift the outboard off the pushpit bracket (or out of the cockpit locker) and carefully lay it in the bottom of the tender. Make sure you are in a secure position and everything is steady before attempting to lift the outboard onto the bracket at the back of the tender. This should be fairly easy with a small 2hp outboard, but gets progressively more and more difficult with outboards in excess of 4hp. Screw up the clamps as tightly as possible. If there is a leash, secure it to the tender. An outboard can jump off the stern with no warning – without a leash, you will never see it again!

- Make sure the outboard has a full tank with the fuel. Open the air vent on top of the tank. The outboard may need choke with the twist-grip in the 'Start' position. The gear shift should be in neutral.
- You must attach the red KILL CORD to your thigh or wrist before starting the

Lifting an outboard on and off the tender involves a balancing act – make sure you don't let go!

engine. The kill cord will cut the engine if you fall over the side.
- When pulling the starter cord, check behind first. Don't pull right back and hit a fellow crew in the face! A short, sharp pull should be all that is required to start a modern outboard.
- Once the engine is running, check that a stream of cooling water is coming out of the engine leg.
- Move the gearshift slowly between neutral, forward and reverse gears.

Always read the owner's manual before using the outboard.

15

PROPELLERS ARE DANGEROUS

- Always wear a kill cord.
- Keep your speed down.
- Beware of other water users. Keep well clear of swimmers. If you get close, cut the engine and use the oars.
- When you leave the beach, do not start the engine with anyone standing in the water close to the propeller.
- An inflatable tender powered by an outboard is not a children's toy boat. Whilst it is important to ensure your children are able to operate a tender safely, leaving them unsupervised to lark around in a tender with an outboard is dangerous and unwise.

ON SHORE

- Be ready to cut the engine and pull the outboard leg up when you reach shallow water. Do not risk breaking a shear-pin if the propeller hits the bottom.
- Never drag an inflatable tender over the ground. Always lift and carry if you want it to last more than a few years.
- Leave the tender in a sensible position, which will not inconvenience other people. Propellers, anchors and painters are annoying and potentially dangerous – particularly for children – when carelessly left on a beach.

"Walkies!" Make sure the tide is not rising before you leave that tender…

15

IN THE DARK

A lot of people have had this experience. You go ashore in the tender, enjoy an evening ashore, climb back in, head back out and can't find your yacht. The combination of a crowded anchorage and dark night can be very perplexing!

- Make sure you leave the anchor light on.
- Consider leaving the saloon light on.
- Make a visual record of where your yacht is located. If it helps, take bearings with a hand-bearing compass or record the position on a hand-held GPS.

TOWING A TENDER

You are asking for trouble towing a small inflatable tender with an outboard attached. You may get away with it, towing at slow speed on flat water, but waves and wind will be ready to flip that tender upside-down. It's much more sensible to stow the outboard on the yacht. For the same reason, remove the oars and anything loose in the tender.

Painter length is critical when towing a small, inflatable tender. If the painter is too long, the inflatable will start veering from side to side when the yacht picks up speed. It may also gradually fill up with water splashing over the bows, with the prospect of increased

Always tow a tender on a short painter which will help lift the bows.

weight ripping the painter from the tender.

The only way to pull the painter in is to completely stop the boat. You will be amazed that there is a big load on that line, even at 2–3 knots. A short painter – possibly 1–2 metres maximum – will let the inflatable ride on its stern with the bows lifted well clear of the water. It may be beneficial to open the drain plug in the transom for towing.

TRUE STORY

Always carry a white light at night. So many people zip about in total darkness, with the weird belief that god is watching over all inflatable tenders. This is just not true, as the following story illustrates:

Two young guys set out from their yachts on a dark night in a beautiful Caribbean anchorage. Both have small, well-powered inflatables, good for about 15 knots. Neither have lights. They collide at full speed. One guys falls over the side. He didn't bother to connect the kill cord to his wrist or leg, so the engine just keeps going at full throttle, with the unmanned inflatable turning in tighter and tighter circles. Eventually the propeller runs straight over his head. Surprisingly, it didn't kill him, but he still has deep scars to remind him of this true story, thanks to two fundamental mistakes:

No kill cord.
No light.

15

KEEPING A TENDER ON DECK

When launching a tender or pulling it back onto the foredeck, it helps to use a halyard to lift it over the guardrails.

An inflatable tender can normally be stowed upside-down on the foredeck between the forestay and mast. You need to make sure it is extremely well tied down and totally secure – any strong wind will funnel underneath and try to lift the tender off the deck when your are sailing or motoring. Beware that a tender can also lift off if vicious squalls hit an anchorage in the middle of the night, which can happen unexpectedly in the Mediterranean.

There are two big advantages of stowing a tender on the foredeck. First, you don't have to worry about losing the tender when you're towing and get caught by strong winds. Second, you don't have to go through all the hassle of deflation and disassembly, followed by inflation and assembly at the next anchorage. There are also several disadvantages. It's difficult to access the foredeck for anchoring and mooring. The tender covers the forehatch and makes the forecabin very dark. Pointed sterns of a tender have a fatal attraction for catching headsail sheets when you tack. The tender obscures the view and means the helmsman has to stand. If the tender has a protruding anchor bracket, use some padding to avoid scratching the forehatch or deck.

1 Fully deflated and carefully rolled, an inflatable tender will fit in a cockpit locker.

2 Roll out the tender and inflate the chambers on the coachroof or foredeck.

3 As an alternative to manhandling, the main halyard makes it easy to lift the tender in or out of the water.

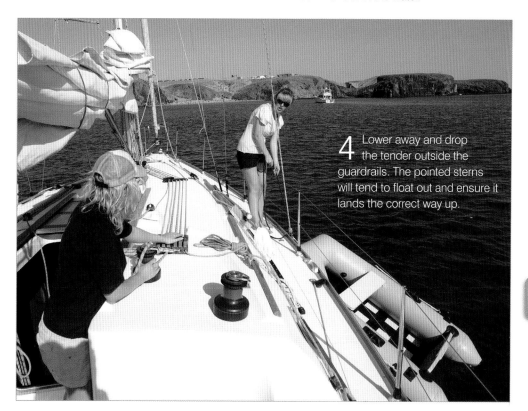

4 Lower away and drop the tender outside the guardrails. The pointed sterns will tend to float out and ensure it lands the correct way up.

15

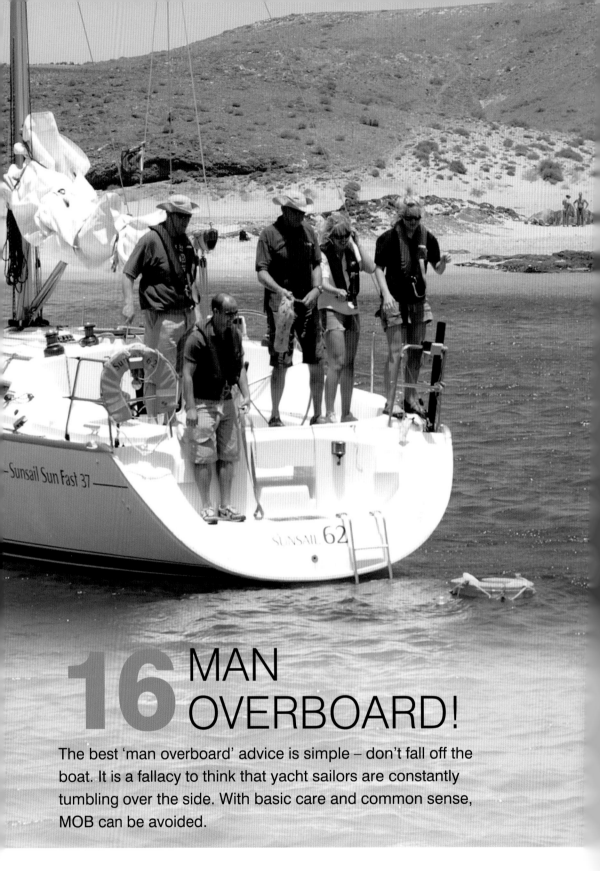

16 MAN OVERBOARD!

The best 'man overboard' advice is simple – don't fall off the boat. It is a fallacy to think that yacht sailors are constantly tumbling over the side. With basic care and common sense, MOB can be avoided.

Causes of Man Overboard:

Most MOB situations are caused by complacency, poor weather conditions or a combination of the two. It is just as easy to fall overboard when you are motoring in flat water on a sunny day as it is sailing to windward in a Force 7. Common sense and caution should be applied at all times!

HOW TO AVOID AN MOB SITUATION

- Stay in the cockpit, particularly in rough weather and at night.

- Wear a harness and clip on securely in rough weather or poor visibility.

- 'One hand for yourself and one for the boat.' The old seamen knew best. Always hold on when moving around the boat. If you are moving along the decks, stay low for best balance and always move along the high (or windward) side of the boat.

- Beware tacks and gybes. Clear the decks and stay in the cockpit for tacks and gybes. The helm must inform all the crew before making any major change in course. This includes any tight turns in a marina.

- Do not pee off the boat, either off the stern or off the side. It is much safer to go below and use the heads. If there is a problem, use a bucket in the cockpit.

16

MAN OVERBOARD PRACTICE

Despite the fact that it will hopefully never happen, all the crew should practise man overboard recovery drills. Apart from being an important safety procedure, it's a great way to improve boat handling. Man Overboard drills play an important role in the RYA Day Skipper course, when the normal 'test' method is to suddenly chuck a fender off the stern! The object is to retrieve the man overboard safely and without delay. Survival in cold water is only possible for a limited time.

There are different theories on how best to respond to a Man Overboard, with different courses of action for different situations, all of which have the same guidelines:

■ Yell "Man overboard!" to alert the crew

and throw the lifebuoy and its attachments (light, danbuoy and drogue) off the stern.

■ One crew member should keep pointing at the man overboard, so he isn't lost from sight during the confusion of dropping sails and changing course. Take a bearing on the man overboard.

■ Press the DSC distress alert on the VHF radio and MOB alarm on the GPS to record the yacht's position.

■ Start the engine, drop the headsail and change course for the recovery. Brief the crew.

■ Make a Mayday call on Channel 16. Notify the emergency services as soon as the man overboard is recovered.

1 "Man overboard!" The horseshoe and danbuoy are thrown towards the person in the water, with one crew pointing to maintain visual contact.

2 Having grabbed the line attached to the horseshoe and danbuoy, the man overboard can be pulled in towards the stern.

3 This mock 'MOB' makes clear that rescuing a man overboard would be a serious challenge with the yacht manoeuvering in wind and waves.

4 No problem getting back on board in flat water, but an exhausted man overboard could find it impossible to climb onto a yacht pitching in waves.

16

MAN OVERBOARD STRATEGIES

MOB REACH-TO-REACH RESCUE.

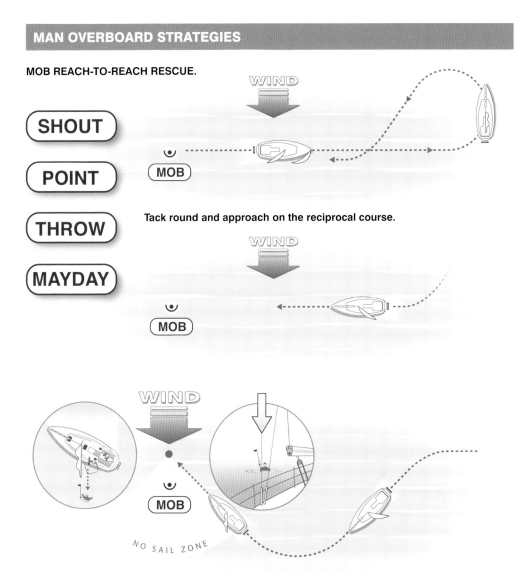

SHOUT

POINT

THROW

MAYDAY

Tack round and approach on the reciprocal course.

On the final approach, bear away and then head up onto a close reach, so you can drift towards the MOB with sails flapping.

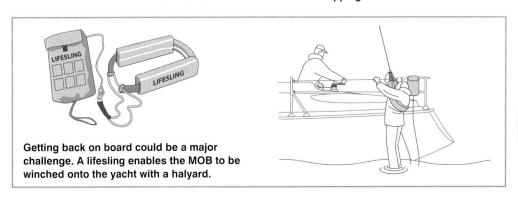

Getting back on board could be a major challenge. A lifesling enables the MOB to be winched onto the yacht with a halyard.

16

SURVIVAL IN THE SEA

If you are unlucky enough to fall off a yacht, inflate your lifejacket to keep your head above water.

- Use the lifejacket light and whistle to attract attention.
- If a lifebuoy has been thrown, try to grab the line that attaches it to the yacht.
- Cover your nose and mouth to avoid swallowing water.
- The greatest danger is likely to be cold water. Cross your legs and wrap your arms tightly around your body. Close wrist, ankle and neck fastenings on clothing.

PICKING UP THE MAN OVERBOARD

Under sail
- Sail away from the man overboard on a beam reach and furl or drop the headsail.
- Tack and bear away onto a beam reach.
- Make the final approach on a close reach. This will allow you to head up, or bear away to position the boat appropriately.

Under engine
- Recovery under engine is recommended unless circumstances prevent it e.g. ropes in the water.
- Tack immediately with headsail cleated, so the yacht is hove-to.
- Throw a heaving line if the man overboard is close by.
- If that fails, start the engine and furl the headsail.
- Centre the mainsail and sheet it in as tight as possible.
- Motor through a semi-circle to approach the man overboard close reach.
- Keep the yacht between the wind and the MOB – this will ensure that as you stop the yacht will be blown towards the casualty.

EMERGENCY

Rescue by sea or air

When a lifeboat approaches, the coxswain will need to talk to the crew on VHF. It is vital that the lifeboat does not foul ropes or rigging in the water. The yacht crew must follow the coxswain's instructions. If the yacht is taken in tow, attach the rope to strong foredeck cleats and back up with rope led aft to the primary winches. Beware of chafe if the tow rope passes through the bow roller.

When a rescue helicopter approaches, listen for instructions on VHF. You will not be able to hear when the helicopter is overhead. You may use red hand-held or orange smoke to attract attention, but do not fire parachute flares when a helicopter is nearby. Keep the yacht on a steady course as instructed. To lift off crew, a helicopter will normally drop a winch wire by the stern of the yacht. Allow the wire to hit the water and 'earth' before you reach for it. Do not attach the wire to the yacht.

16

EMERGENCY ESSENTIALS

- A lifebuoy is stowed on the pushpit where it can be thrown towards a man overboard. It should be marked with the yacht's name and reflective tape. Fittings should include a whistle, automatic light and drogue to prevent drift.
- A danbuoy is a day-glo flag on a pole linked to the lifebuoy. It is designed to be visible 2 metres above the water to help spot the location of a man overboard.
- Emergency Position Indicating Radio Beacons (EPIRBs) transmit a distress position signal as part of the Global Maritime Distress and Safety System (GMDSS). They are activated manually or automatically by hydrostatic release. On longer offshore races, each crew will be given a personal EPIRB to carry on deck.

GETTING THE MAN OVERBOARD BACK ON THE YACHT

Normal advice is to approach to windward of the man overboard. This will provide some protection from waves. If the yacht is heeling, the leeward side deck will be closer to the water, but the yacht could be pushed over the top of the man overboard in strong winds.

- Climbing onto the stern is theoretically easiest. However, this could be difficult and dangerous when the stern is rising and falling in a sea.
- Some kind of lifting gear, using a halyard, may be required to pull the casualty up from the water. An MOB casualty will be significantly heavier than their normal weight due to the weight of their wet clothing.
- The man overboard may be suffering from hypothermia. Get him below out of the wind and wet clothes and preferably into a sleeping bag. Call the emergency services for medical assistance if required.

TAKE A COURSE

RYA Sea Survival

One-day course on how to survive in an emergency includes preparation for sea survival, lifejackets, liferaft session in a swimming pool, search and rescue.

USING A LIFE-RAFT

Abandoning a yacht is the last resort. It is normally much safer to stay on board, unless the yacht is in immediate danger of sinking or fire is out of control.

- Only launch the life-raft if you have decided to abandon the yacht.
- The static line must be attached to the yacht before the life-raft is lifted off the yacht and dropped in the sea. Pull the static line to start inflation.
- A life-raft will rock around on the waves. Heavier crew should get in first to provide stability. Seasickness may be a major problem.
- Take the grab bag with emergency equipment before leaving the yacht. Depending on what is stored inside the life-raft, contents could include a hand-held VHF, EPIRB, flares, first aid kit, torch, water, emergency food and thermal protection.

READ A BOOK

RYA Sea Survival Handbook (G43) by Keith Colwell

All you need to know about preparing to go to sea, emergency procedures, safety equipment, life-saving signals, handling heavy weather and choosing the most suitable lifejacket or buoyancy aid.

16

17 WHERE TO ENJOY YACHT CRUISING

Cruising offers limitless possibilities. Tierra del Fuego? No doubt it could be a wonderful sailing area, so long as the weather is OK! Back down to earth, here is a personal selection of beautiful places to sail and explore on a yacht, starting with Scotland.

SCOTLAND

Scotland provides a superb cruising ground with a massive choice of bays, inlets and islands along its entire length, including the Hebrides to the north-west. It is rugged, magnificent and lightly populated with mountains providing a dramatic backdrop to the scenery. The weather can be wild, with tidal races and whirlpools providing a real challenge for navigators. However, that is only part of the picture. Areas such as the Firth of Clyde and Sound of Bute are completely protected from the open ocean, so that it feels like you are sailing on an inland sea with moderate tide and plenty of safe harbours close by. The marina on the outskirts of the small, attractive town of Largs provides an excellent gateway to cruising this area. Further north, everyone should cruise through the Caledonian Canal at least once. This magnificent route links the west and east coasts of Scotland and provides the opportunity to sail the 26 mile length of the infamous Loch Ness!

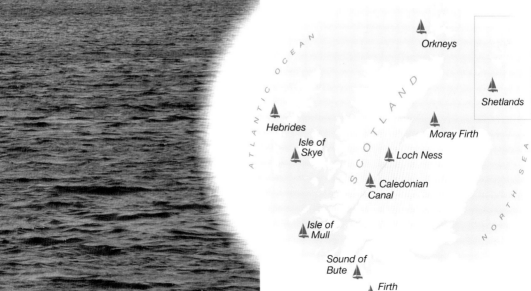

17

THE SOLENT

Britain is a great sailing nation, but take the weather as you find it and be prepared to deal with fast flowing tides. The Solent provides a thrilling compact cruising area in central southern England, which is well protected from the open sea, but can get extremely crowded in high season. Distances between the mainland and the Isle of Wight are short, with a great choice of interesting places to visit including Yarmouth, Lymington, Portsmouth Harbour, Bembridge and the yacht racing mecca of Cowes, which should be avoided like the plague during 'Cowes Week' in the first week of August!

Beware of the infamous 'Solent chop' when wind blows against tide, watch the depth under your keel and keep a keen lookout for other vessels, particularly ferries and ships using the main channels for Southampton and Portsmouth. For something really special, take a trip up the Beaulieu River. To avoid the crowds, try sailing on a weekday in winter when the Solent can be absolutely beautiful.

Southampton

Beaulieu
River

Portsmouth
Harbour

THE SOLENT

Cowes

Yarmouth

Bembridge

ISLE OF
WIGHT

17

The Solent provides a challenging compact cruising area in central southern England, which is well protected from the open sea.

17

FINLAND AND THE SWEDISH ARCHIPELAGO

The Baltic Sea between Finland and Sweden provides a superb cruising area with hundreds of islands and inlets scattered around the coast. There is no tide apart from wind-driven currents between the islands and the sea has very low salinity, with plenty of protection in the lee of the land and a huge choice of anchorages where normal practice is to secure the stern of the yacht to a rock or tree on the shore! With no law of trespass you can land virtually anywhere you want in this exceptionally peaceful cruising area, but do not intrude on people's privacy. The main hazard to navigation is underwater rocks – when sailing through narrow channels it is vital to read the chart accurately and navigate carefully. The cruising season is short in this area. June is a beautiful month with plenty of birds, but can still be very cold despite virtual 24 hour daylight. July is warm, but the harbours are at their busiest as most Finns are on holiday this month. August is much quieter and still warm, but with some risk of algae in the water.

17

The Baltic Sea between Finland and Sweden provides a superb cruising area with hundreds of islands and inlets scattered around the coast.

17

THE FRENCH-ITALIAN TRIANGLE

Sailing past Monaco, Menton, Villefranche and Cannes provides a wonderful once-in-a-lifetime yacht cruising experience, but beware that marinas can become impossibly crowded during the summer and very expensive. The Iles de Lerins and Iles d'Hyeres are particularly attractive, largely unspoilt and provide some good anchorages. There are no tides in the Mediterranean, but the winds can be tricky – either too little when you have to motor everywhere, or too much when you have to flee for shelter from the northerly Mistral, which can be very strong.

About 90 miles to the south of the Cote d'Azur, the island of Corsica is perfect for a two-week circumnavigation. Its high hills and mountains look superb from the sea, but too many boats in high season and big rolling waves may diminish your pleasure. The Bonifacio Straits at the southern end of Corsica are particularly fine, with a charming small chain of islands leading to the northern end of Sardinia. Further east, the Italian islands of Capraia and Giglio are delightful, but are best visited out of the main holiday season.

Mistral Winds

FRANCE

Nice
Cannes
Iles de Lerins
Marseille
Iles d'Hyeres
Cote d' Azur
Capraia
Corsica
ITALY
Balearic Islands
Giglio
Sardinia
MEDITERRANEAN SEA
Sicily
NORTH AFRICA

17

The Aeolian Islands, on the south-west coast of Italy within sight of Sicily, provide wonderful cruising within a volcanic landscape.

17

EASTERN MEDITERRANEAN

Croatia offers an extensive tide-free cruising ground on the east side of the Adriatic, with fine old towns to visit and beautiful buildings built for the area's former Venetian rulers. There are more than a thousand islands along the shoreline, with the Kornati Islands allowing superb cruising in a designated national park with minimal tourist development.

Greece offers wonderful cruising on two major seas. The Ionian stretches to the south of Corfu with Paxos, Anti-Paxos, Levkas, Ithaca and Cephalonia offering a truly Homeric sailing experience. The sea-breeze can get fresh on summer afternoons, but conditions are normally pleasant with plenty of shelter in the lee of the islands. On the eastern side of the Corinth Canal, the Aegean Sea is where Greece meets Turkey – the sea can become rough with the Meltemi blowing hard on hot afternoons. This is an immense cruising area littered with delightful islands, ranging from Santorini in the south to Lemnos and Thassos in the north.

Neigbouring Turkey provides similar conditions. The most popular stretch of coast between Bodrum and Marmaris has become over-developed, but there are still some very pleasant small harbours and bays. The east Lycian coast between Fethiye and Anatalya is particularly interesting, with some extraordinary ancient ruins. This is a delightful area, if you can escape the water-borne touts and gulets which flood the coast in high season. Beware that both Greece and Turkey can become unpleasantly hot in July and August, even when afloat. June and September are likely to be more temperate and a lot less crowded.

17

Turkey combines ancient civilisation with modern cruising, enabling you to moor up in some fascinating historic locations.

17

CANARY ISLANDS

The chain of Canary Islands off the coast of West Africa makes an unusual cruising ground, with the possibility of getting pleasant sailing weather year-round although the area can get hit by strong winds and big, rolling seas. Deep water and rocky coastlines mean there are not many places where you can drop anchor, but the islands are magnificent when viewed from the sea, which also has the advantage of being almost tide-free.

For sailors, the busiest time of year is the run-up to autumn when yachts arrive, prior to crossing the Atlantic to the Caribbean. Otherwise, the Canaries is a very quiet cruising area and sailing downwind through the island chain of Lanzarote, Fuerteventura, Gran Canaria, Tenerife, La Gomera and El Hierro offers great cruising potential. Unfortunately, it's a rough bash to windward in the opposite direction!

Trade Winds

ATLANTIC OCEAN

La Palma

Lanzarote

Tenerife

Fuerteventura

La Gomera

El Hierro

Gran Canaria

ATLANTIC OCEAN

17

Sailing between Lanzarote and Fuerteventura at the eastern end of the Canary Islands in perfect cruising weather, which can be experienced any time of year.

17

BRITISH VIRGIN ISLANDS

The British Virgin Islands, near the top of the Caribbean island chain, are one of the world's most popular cruising grounds for bareboat sailing holidays. A cluster of islands and islets provide a delightful cruising area that's just 32 miles long and half as wide, enjoying a wonderful climate with 24–31C average temperatures throughout the year. A fortnight would be perfect to explore all that the BVI can offer at a relaxed pace, including a visit to the 'sunken island' of Anegada, which is surrounded by a coral reef and 14 miles distant from the main group.

Sailing in the BVI is crew-friendly for all levels of skill. You can be anywhere in the islands within a few hours. Force 3–5 Trade Winds normally ensure you can sail every day. Minimal tides and line of sight navigation make it straightforward to find your way around the maze of islands, with the Sir Francis Drake Channel providing a passage between the islands, well protected from the prevailing easterly swell. The BVI have a huge choice of anchorages, most of which have mooring buoys for visitors to prevent yachts anchoring on top of fragile coral.

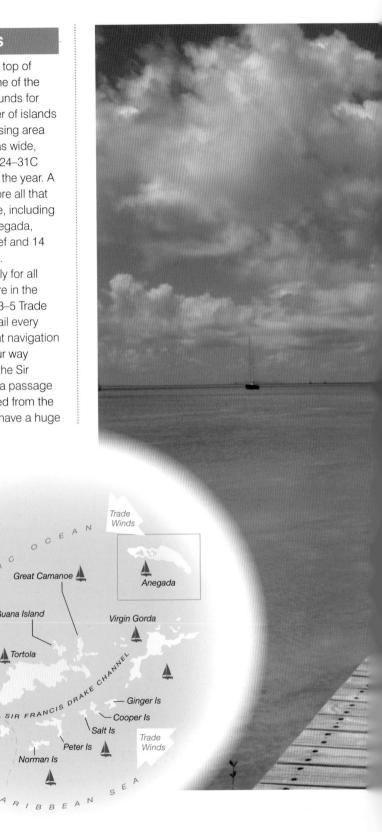

Trade Winds

ATLANTIC OCEAN

Great Camanoe

Anegada

Guana Island

Virgin Gorda

Jost Van Dyke

Tortola

SIR FRANCIS DRAKE CHANNEL

Ginger Is

Cooper Is

Salt Is

Trade Winds

Peter Is

St John
U.S.
Virgin Islands

Norman Is

CARIBBEAN SEA

17

A fortnight would be perfect to explore all that the BVI can offer at a relaxed pace.

17

YACHT CHARTER

All of the cruising areas featured in this section have plenty of options for yacht charter. Your first choice is whether to opt for bareboat or flotilla…

Flotilla cruising is a brilliant concept, which is particularly suited to novice sailors but also appeals to experienced crews who enjoy the concept of cruising in company. A small fleet of identical yachts cruise around a carefully selected area on a one or two-week flotilla. The lead boat is normally staffed by a skipper, hostess and mechanic. Each morning the skipper gives a full briefing on how to reach the next destination. Yachts may choose their own route, cruising alone or in company. When they arrive, the lead boat will be waiting to help with mooring, which can be the most stressful element of yacht cruising in a new area. The hostess will help with provisioning and entertainments, such as barbecues for the whole fleet. The mechanic will fix any problems with the yachts. Flotillas are suitable for all levels of ability. Novice crews can enjoy one-week flotillas in lighter wind cruising

areas, with companies such as Neilson (www.neilson.com) providing specialist 3-day intensive tuition courses immediately before the start of a flotilla, backed up by the expertise of the lead boat crew who are always on call. Flotilla holidays can be enjoyed in the Solent, Croatia, Greece, Turkey and the British Virgin Islands.

Bareboat cruising is like car hire – you rent a yacht and take it away, normally for a

17

one-week or two-week cruise. Experience is obviously required. At the very least, the skipper will need to have completed an RYA Day Skipper course or be able to prove their ability, with one or two crew preferably at RYA Competent Crew level. An option is to hire a skipper who will live on board and manage the boat, which makes it possible to enjoy bareboat cruising with a novice crew. This will tend to work best with larger yachts in excess of 12 metres (40 feet) LOA (length overall).

The costs of bareboat cruising will include a fee for hiring the yacht, insurance and fuel, plus mooring charges for each night away. Companies such as Sunsail (www.sunsail.com) and The Moorings (www.moorings.com) charter bareboats world-wide, with particular emphasis on the Mediterranean and Caribbean, while a search on the internet will provide choices of bareboats for cruising the Solent, West Coast of Scotland or Scandinavia.

GLOSSARY

Apparent wind – Wind experienced when a boat is moving.

Bareboat – Chartering a yacht without skipper or crew.

Barometer – Measures barometric pressure and predicts stormy weather.

Battens – Plastic 'stiffeners' in the mainsail.

Beating – Sailing as close to the wind as possible.

Beaufort – The Beaufort Scale is measured as Force 1, Force 2, etc.

Bend – Knot that ties two ropes together.

Bimini – Cockpit cover to protect crew from the sun.

Binnacle – Pedestal for compass, usually with a wheel.

Block – Roller for rope control lines such as halyard and sheets.

Bow roller – Heavy duty stainless steel fitting in the bow which lets you pay out the anchor chain.

Cardinal marks – Buoys or markers indicating the safe side on which to pass a hazard or obstruction.

Channel 16 – International distress frequency for maritime use.

Chart table – The chart table area is the navigation zone, normally with space for a paper chart.

Charter – Hiring a yacht.

Cleats – Horn-shaped fittings to secure a rope.

Clew – Corner of a sail attached to the sheet.

Clutches – Locking devices for halyards and control lines.

Coachroof – Raised roof to allow standing headroom down below.

Cockpit – Main crew area when under way.

Code Flag V – "I require assistance."

Companionway – Main entrance to the saloon, galley and navigation areas.

Competent Crew – Popular RYA course to learn crew skills.

Cruising chute – Loose luff sail with a full shape for broad reaching downwind.

Danbuoy – Marker buoy incorporating flag on a tall rod for man overboard.

Day Skipper – RYA course for basic yacht skipper skills.

DSC – Digital Selective Calling on VHF radio.

Ensign – National flag flown at the stern. The Red Ensign is flown by most British yachts.

EPIRB – Emergency Position Indicating Radio Beacon.

Fairleads – A lead for a rope, such as a fairlead in the toerail for a mooring warp.

Fairway buoy – Safe water mark at the start of a channel.

Fender – Protects the side of a boat when alongside.

Fiddles – Sliders to lock pans or kettles on the top of a stove.

Flotilla – Group of yachts which sail in company. Very popular as yachting holidays with professional lead boat crew.

Fluke – The part of an anchor that holds in sand, mud or whatever is on the bottom.

Foot – The bottom of a sail.

Foredeck – Front deck between bow and mast.

Forestay – Rigging wire (normally) supporting mast from the front.

Furling headsail – Headsail that rolls up when not in use or when reefed.

Galley – Yacht's kitchen area.

Genoa – Headsail which overlaps mast and mainsail.

Gimbals – Pivot which allows galley cooker to change angle and stay level as the boat heels.

GMDSS – Global Maritime Distress and Safety System.

Gooseneck – Join between mast and boom.

GPS – Global Positioning System.

Guardrails – Horizontal wires around the sides of the boat, supported by stanchions.

Gybing – Turning the stern of the boat through the direction the wind is blowing from (bearing away), causing the boom to swing to the new side.

Head – Top corner of a sail.

Heads – Yacht's WC and bathroom area.

Headsail – Sail in front of the mast.

Hitch – Knot that ties rope to a ring or post.

Horseshoe buoy – Semi-circular flotation device for assisting a man overboard.

IALA – International Association of Lighthouse Authorities.

Isophase – Equal light and dark flashes from a lighthouse or navigation mark.

Jackstays – Webbing or wires for secure harness attachment when moving along the side decks.

Jamming cleat – Cleat fitted with jamming 'jaws'. Typical use includes mainsheet which often has a powerful spring-loaded jamming cleat.

Jib – Small headsail with clew in front of the mast.

Kicker – Used to hold the boom down when the mainsheet is eased for reaching or running. Also called kicking strap or vang.

Kill cord – Kills the ignition of an outboard motor if you fall out of the tender. Use it!

Knots – 1 knot = 1 nautical mile per hour.

Lateral marks – Buoys or markers showing the sides of a channel.

Lazy line – Line on the dock attached to a mooring warp linked to a seabed mooring. Widely used in the Mediterranean for stern-to berthing.

Lazyjacks – Spider's web of light lines between mast and boom used to catch the mainsail as it drops.

Lee helm – The yacht keeps trying to bear away from the wind, which indicates it is out of balance.

Leech – Trailing edge of sail.

Leeward – Where the wind is blowing to.

Lowers – Wires (normally) supporting side-bend in the mast below the main spreaders.

Luff – Leading edge of sail.

Mainsail – Sail that sets on the mast.

Mainsheet – Rope used to control the horizontal angle of the boom and mainsail.

Mayday – Grave and imminent danger requiring immediate assistance.

MMSI – Maritime Mobile Service Identity.

Nautical mile – 1 nautical mile = 1.25 statute miles.

Occulting – More light than dark.

Pan Pan – Urgent message.

Port – Red. Left side of boat.

Port tack – Sailing with the wind blowing onto the port side of the boat.

Pulpit – Fixed stainless steel rails around the bow.

Pushpit – Fixed stainless steel rails around the stern.

Reaching – Sailing with the wind blowing from the side.

Reefing – Reducing sail area.

Reefing cringle – Stainless steel eyes used for pulling down reefs in luff and leech of mainsail.

Reefing pennant – Reefing lines led through cringles.

Riding turn – Locked rope on a winch due to over-riding turns.

Running – Sailing with the wind behind you.

Sail ties – Short lengths of rope or webbing used to secure a folded mainsail on the boom.

Saloon – Main cabin.

SART – Search and Rescue Transponder.

Sea strainer – Raw water filter for engine cooling.

Sector lights – Green, white, red.

Securité – Navigational safety message.

Self-tailing winch – Winch with locking jaws to hold rope while you wind.

Shank – Main arm of an anchor.

Sheet – Rope used to control sail trim.

Shrouds – Rigging wire (normally) supporting mast from the sides.

Spinnaker – Triangular sail with a full shape for running downwind.

Spreaders – Struts to control side-bend of mast.

Spring – Rope used to prevent a yacht moving backwards or forwards when moored alongside.

Stack-pack – Mainsail bag with full length zipper, which is permanently fitted to the boom.

Stanchions – Stainless steel posts to support guardrails round the side of a yacht.

Starboard – Green. Right side of boat.

Starboard tack – Sailing with the wind blowing onto the starboard side of the boat.

Stop cocks – Valves fitted to the through-hull fittings.

Tack – Front corner of a sail which is in a fixed position.

Tacking – Turning the bow of the boat through the direction the wind is blowing from (heading up), causing the boom to swing to the new side.

Toerail – Shallow aluminium or wooden rail around the side of the boat, following the line where the deck is joined to the hull.

Topping lift – Control line used to support the end of the boom when the mainsail is not hoisted.

Track – Sliding aluminium track typically used to vary sheeting angle of mainsheet or headsail sheets.

Transom – The back of the boat.

True wind – The wind you feel when the boat is stationary.

Turning blocks – Blocks used to turn control lines through a change in direction, for instance when led from the mast to the cockpit via the coachroof.

Uppers – Wires (normally) supporting side-bend in the mast above the main spreaders.

Vang – see Kicker.

VHF Radio – Very High Frequency (VHF) radio is your main and most reliable means of communication on a small vessel at sea.

Warp – Rope used to move a boat.

Waypoints – Locations that are entered into your GPS to assist with passage planning.

Weather helm – The yacht keeps trying to head up towards the wind, which indicates it is not well balanced.

Winch – Device used to provide mechanical advantage when pulling on sheets or halyards.

Windlass – Winch used to drop and lift anchor chain.

Windward – Where the wind is blowing from.

INDEX

RYA Training Courses
for all ages, abilities and aspirations

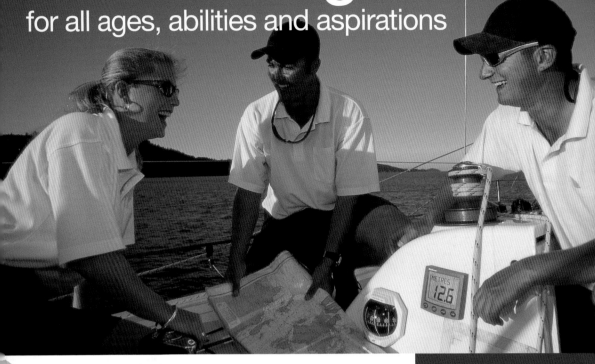

> Get the most from your time on the water with our range of practical and shorebased courses.

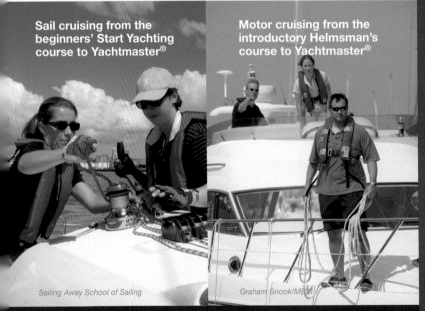

Sail cruising from the beginners' Start Yachting course to Yachtmaster®

Motor cruising from the introductory Helmsman's course to Yachtmaster®

Sailing Away School of Sailing

Graham Snook/MBM

Also, a whole range of navigation and specialist short courses:

> **ESSENTIAL NAVIGATION AND SEAMANSHIP**

> **DAY SKIPPER**

> **COASTAL SKIPPER/ YACHTMASTER® OFFSHORE**

> **YACHTMASTER® OCEAN**

> **DIESEL ENGINE**

> **OFFSHORE SAFETY**

> **VHF RADIO**

> **RADAR**

> **SEA SURVIVAL**

> **FIRST AID**

For further information see www.rya.org.uk, call 00 44 (0)23 8060 4158 for a brochure or email training@rya.org.uk